Advance Praise for *The Book o...*

"Read this book! I absolutely love it. Annie Korzen... ... humanity are a treasure."

  —Joey Soloway, screenwriter and director, *Transparent*

"Annie's stories have made me feel all the feelings while laughing and wishing I could have been there for all of them. Well... most of them."

  —Debbie Jhoon, screenwriter, *Mafia Mamma*

"Annie Korzen is funny, inspirational, provocative, and authentic. She has perfected the art of complaining without being annoying. Life is a bit brighter because Annie is in it, and this book is perfect for those who want to see the world through her eyes."

  —Wayne Federman, author, *The History of Stand-up*

"This book will brighten your day. It's hilarious and sprinkled with moments of real insight."

  —Annabelle Gurwitch, *New York Times*
  bestselling author, *I See You Made an Effort*

"Annie Korzen is a master storyteller, and her book is hilarious, warm, wise, and brutally honest. Even if you can't sit across from her in real life, you can dig into this delicious book."

  —Catherine Burns, artistic director, The Moth

"She'll stop at nothing until it's funny. Or poignant. Or memorable. What a treat!"

  —Treva Silverman, Emmy award–winning writer,
  The Mary Tyler Moore Show

"Annie Korzen is entertaining, profound, and compassionate. She should rule the world. (Also, she made me write this.)"

  —Jonathan Korzen, son

THE BOOK OF ANNIE

Humor, Heart, and Chutzpah from an Accidental Influencer

ANNIE KORZEN

A PERMUTED PRESS BOOK

ISBN: 979-8-88845-058-1
ISBN (eBook): 979-8-88845-059-8

The Book of Annie:
Humor, Heart, and Chutzpah from an Accidental Influencer
© 2023 by Annie Korzen
All Rights Reserved

Cover art by Jim Villaflores

Permuted Press, LLC
New York • Nashville
permutedpress.com

Published in the United States of America
1 2 3 4 5 6 7 8 9 10

To Mackenzie, who gave me a new life

CONTENTS

AUTHOR'S NOTE

I have this problem: I don't really know what it is that I do. I'm funny, but I'm not a comic, because some of my stuff gets emotional. I'm a storyteller, but I hate that word because it sounds so "folksy" and I am definitely not a country gal. So I guess what I am is a humorist—which means that I am a proud member of a profession that does not exist. The last humorist I heard of was Mark Twain, and he was pretty good. He was the one who said, "The older I get, the more clearly I remember things that never happened."

At my advanced age, eighty-three as I write this, I've suddenly found a huge new audience for my work. Several hundred thousand people on TikTok seem to think I'm funny, wise, and inspiring. I hope they're right, because I've decided to share my thoughts in this book.

So, here are some stories, anecdotes, and random observations—some from my previous life in New York, others from my many years of exile in L.A. I hope these musings will not only make you laugh, but also make you a better human being, because, wonderful as you already are, we can all benefit from an occasional upgrade. In any case, you may as well enjoy it because if you don't, I'm not giving refunds. By the way, everything in this book is absolutely true—except for the stuff I made up.

Some of you younger readers may not be familiar with every movie, show, actor, or writer that I mention. It might behoove you to look them up, because chances are, they are worth knowing.

P.S. A few of these stories have been adapted from pieces originally published in AARP's *The Ethel* newsletter. They are either much longer or much shorter here, with many added obscenities.

1

HAPPINESS

How do you get it, and is it really necessary?

They say that true happiness comes not from wealth and celebrity, but from spending time with people you love and who love you. Personally, I'd rather be rich and famous, but while I'm waiting for that to happen, I try to enjoy what I've got.

Happiness, in case you were wondering, is a good thing, not just for you but also for the rest of us. Unhappy people are mean to others, and we don't need more mean people in the world. (Happiness is also supposed to be good for your health, but I'm not sure about that one. I can think of lots of mean, angry, and miserable people who manage to stay alive year after year after year. Need I name names?)

So how do we get happy? One thing I know for sure is that we can never predict exactly how things will turn out; there's no scientific formula for that. The only thing to do is to try everything and see what works. My mantra is, "Yeah, why not?"

There are, however, some basic necessities for a good life:

A comfy home.

Satisfying work.

Hanging out with fun people.

Spaghetti. Lots of spaghetti.

Here's what you do not need for a happy life:

A low-carb diet.

Fame. Just look at those dysfunctional royals.

Power. Was Stalin a merry old soul? I doubt it. Possessions. Owning a shitload of stuff that you paid a shitload of money for is no guarantee that you will lead a blissful existence. It might, however, indicate that you are shallow and superficial. (Again, I won't mention any obvious names, in case Melania reads this book and decides to share some surplus wealth with me.)

The thing I hate about life is that everything can change in one moment.

The thing I love about life is that everything can change in one moment.

Some people are better at happiness than others, and they always look on the bright side. I hate those people. I hate them because I wish I could be like them. On the other hand, there is one advantage to being a glass-half-empty person: if you can't see the problem, then you can't fix the problem. Realists get things done. When I ask someone how they are, and they answer, "Oh, you know, can't complain," I always want to say, "Force yourself."

2

RELATIONSHIPS

Friends, lovers, partners, neighbors,
enemies—all that humanoid stuff

Scenes from a Marriage

I am older than most funny ladies, so my issues are a little different from younger women's. Like, I've been married for a katrillion years, so I don't talk about "dating." I think about it, but I don't talk about it.

I met my Danish husband, Benni, on a blind date in February, and we got married in April because he needed a green card. My friends said I was insane to marry a total stranger, that he would get his papers and disappear; but my gut told me that it was real. That was almost sixty years ago, and we're still going strong. Well, maybe "strong" is not the right word, because—big surprise!—our relationship is not perfect. It would be more accurate to say that we're going weak, but at least we're still going.

The worst thing about us is that we bicker constantly. If I say it's too cold in the room, he says, "Oh please, you don't

THE BOOK OF ANNIE

know what you're talking about." If he says there's enough food in the house, I say, "Oh please, you don't know what you're talking about." The sad fact is, Benni and I have very little in common. I like egg rolls and fried rice; he craves liverwurst and herring. I can binge on TV series until the wee hours of the morning; he has news and sports on for hours every day. I like going out; he likes staying in. This might not sound like a blueprint for a happy marriage, but sometimes you have to read between the lines.

I had a solo show that ran for five months, and Benni never missed a performance. And when there are only two cherries left in the bowl, he will leave them for me because he knows I love cherries. He drives me when I don't want to drive (which is always), and he makes dinner when I don't want to cook (which is always). Plus, there's one little thing that we do have in common: he loves me, and I love him, and I guess that counts for something.

Sometimes I'm coming home at night and it's dark and cold, and then I notice a light in our kitchen window, and there's my husband, preparing dinner. At that moment, I get a feeling of what I think is that thing called...happiness.

I admit it: I am often guilty of being a nagging wife. I constantly remind Benni to watch his diet and do his exercises. I guess I'd rather be a nag than a widow.

Dating

It's a much different game now than in my day. I would not have done well with online dating, because I'm much too skeptical. When a guy describes himself as "looking for someone who would like to share fine dining, travel, and theater," I figure the truth is more like warm beer, Burger King, and reality TV. A friend got a phone call from one of these too-good-to-be-true guys. His smooth opening gambit was, "So, how do you feel about Crocs?"

In general, I think single people have unrealistic expectations of perfection in a mate. I fixed up two friends of mine, and it seemed to be going well. Then the woman told me that she needed to end it because he didn't listen to classical music, just jazz. I told her there's nothing wrong with jazz—it's not like he was addicted to the top ten polka albums of all time—and she could go to the opera with her girlfriends. She was smart enough to listen to me, and I danced at their wedding. Why isn't everyone in the world smart enough to listen to me?

> Amy Schumer's husband is on the spectrum. He's a guy; how can she tell?
>
> (In case this book is being reviewed by a guy—I don't mean you.)

Flirting

There are two things you have to do to be popular with men.

1. Let them do all the talking.
2. Laugh at all their jokes, including the dumb ones.

I have never been popular with men.

But one night, at a New York theater party, I decided to practice my flirting. It's not that I was looking for a man; I already had the guy I wanted. But every woman needs appreciation, right?

One of the guests was a middle-aged famous off-Broadway director. His date was a streamlined twenty-one-year-old aerobics instructor whose name was Kelli, with an "I." But Kelli was soon forgotten. I started by asking Famous Director about his career, and I radiated fascination at every word he said. Here's a sample of my end of the conversation: "Uh-huh…uh-huh… uh-huh. Ha, ha, ha, that is *hysterical!*" "Tee-hee-hee, you are *so* funny!" "No! I don't believe it! Then what did you do? That's amazing!" The guy was enchanted by me all evening; no one else could get near him. At the end of the evening, he said, "I really enjoyed talking to you, Franny." Yes, I'm sure he did. And that's how it's done. The question is, is it worth it?

> Every marriage has its little rituals of affection. The morning hug, the goodnight kiss, and the goodbye wave are daily reminders of how lucky you are to be together. Our sweet moment happens at dinner, when Benni and I raise our glasses, look into each other's eyes, and toast each other by saying "skoal." It's a much more pleasant way to end the day than just sitting down and grabbing the saltshaker.

More Scenes from a Marriage

I married a man who hates to buy anything new and hates to throw anything out. For him, stepping into a clothing store is like stepping into the Ninth Circle of Hell. He walks in, grabs a pair of pants without trying them on, and races out the door before I can say, "Look! They're having a sale on cashmere sweaters!"

Benni's wardrobe is a huge jumble of worn-out crappiness, which has led to countless awkward moments. There was the funeral where he paid his respects in a vivid Hawaiian shirt patterned with oversized beer mugs. There was the black-tie event where he showed up in Velcro-strapped bowling shoes. And let us not forget the important business meeting in the soiled bucket hat.

I know there are more important things to worry about, like our divided country and global warming, but I feel powerless about those issues. However, I thought I might actually be able to remedy Benni's weird wardrobe catastrophes.

Here was my plan: I would sneakily remove the worst offenders and replace them with fresh, new, crisp, pieces. But not so fast! There was a moral dilemma here. I knew that if I removed this garbage, Benni would never notice because, unlike me, he does not have an intimate personal acquaintance with every item in his closet. On the other hand, it seemed mean and unwifely to throw his stuff away behind his back. So, I put the mountain of tattered rejects on the bed and asked him to approve my choices. Bad idea. He claimed to be very much attached to the entire lot, and unceremoniously dumped the pile back into the closet.

I tried again. "You have to buy yourself some new clothes."

"Why? I already have clothes."

"You need to wear things that will prevent strangers from offering you spare change, that's why."

He promised to give it some thought. I then cast all morals aside, snuck into his closet, grabbed the worst of the worst, and brought them to the local thrift store. As expected, he never noticed a thing.

The next day, Benni came home, looking very pleased with himself. "Okay, I did it. I went shopping and found a whole lot of stuff that's just perfect for me." He had dropped by the thrift store, and he proudly displayed some Velcro bowling shoes, a soiled bucket hat, and a Hawaiian shirt featuring oversized beer mugs.

Crime does not pay.

On the one hand, I consider myself a feminist. On the other hand, I want a man to take care of me.

Neighbors from Hell

In 1996, we moved into the Fairfax area of Los Angeles, which at that time was an unfashionable neighborhood of old Russian Jews and new Russian immigrants. I liked it because it's one of the few walking neighborhoods in L.A., and I don't want to drive five miles when I need a bunch of kale. (Actually, I never need a bunch of kale, but I think it makes me sound hip— unlike the word "hip.")

Fairfax reminded me of Mosholu Parkway in the Bronx, where I grew up. The fact is, I always hated the Bronx, but it was comforting to find something familiar in the vast and incomprehensible sprawl of L.A.

Shortly after we moved in, I discovered that the family next door were the Neighbors from Hell. The mother, Tillie, couldn't talk without yelling, and the quality of the dialogue was on the level of: "Malina, you have to make a number two before you go to school, so just keep sittin' on da toilet!" This merry banter went on day and night: screaming at her sister on the phone, screaming at her husband in the garage, screaming at their satanic Rottweilers in the backyard.

Little Malina would frequently run away from home (big surprise there) and straight into my garden, with Tillie chasing after her, both yelling at the top of their lungs. This drama would play out right outside my office window as I sat at the computer, desperately trying to find some words to fill up a blank page. "Malina, get back in da house, or I'm gonna call da policeman and he's gonna come and trow you in jail!"

It seemed incarceration was a very real issue for this family. Tillie's brother came for a visit, and he turned out to be an ex-con. His conversation was not only booming; it was down-right scary: "She didn't even fuckin' visit me in jail. If she's fuckin' somebody else, you know I gotta gun!"

So, there I was, a cultured, classy, civilized woman (I drink Aperol spritzes) whose world had been taken over by the Soprano family. I waited for the gangster brother to leave before I dared complain about the noise. Tillie explained, "It's our temperament. We're typical Italian."

Then one day, a sign went up on their front lawn that said, "Palm Readings." Tillie explained, "The truth is, we're Gypsies." (Her word, for the PC watchdogs.) I've always had the stereotypical romantic fantasies about the Romani culture—you know: beautiful, swarthy people, heartbreaking music, sensual dances in which the men applaud their own buttocks. But next door there was no music, no dancing, just hollering.

Tillie was a compulsive housekeeper and an insomniac; so in addition to the constant shrieking, we were usually awakened in the middle of the night by the roar of the vacuum. Her house was indeed spotless. The decor, however, was less than swanky. The living room was dominated by a larger-than-life painting of a bare-chested Arnold Schwarzenegger pointing an Uzi directly at the viewer.

At one of my frequent yard sales, Tillie brought over an almost-new MacBook Pro and asked if we could sell it for her.

"Sure, but you'd get a better price on eBay," I told her.

"No, better not, it might be hot," she said.

I really, really resented these people. I resented having to be part of their chaotic universe of noise, *Terminator* paintings, and hot laptops. I want neighbors who share my respectable, educated, middle-class values. Is that asking too much? Does that make me an entitled, privileged Karen? If so, so be it.

As the years passed, we arrived at a tenuous peace. Malina turned out to be a bright little girl who liked to read, so I occasionally picked up books for her. Things quieted down over there, so I guess Malina finally learned to defecate on command. Tillie was happy to lend extra tables for our yard sales, and if I commented on how good her fried chicken smelled, she insisted on making a plate for me.

By that time, the once-undesirable Fairfax area had become gentrified, and my neighbors couldn't afford the rent increases anymore. They moved into a storefront where Tillie had fortune-telling clients in front; their living area was in the back. Since the Romas moved out, we've had a succession of young executive types. I rarely hear them, I rarely see them, I do not know them. I wouldn't think of ringing their bell to borrow a cup of milk. They probably don't keep milk in the house anyway; they pick up their brown sugar espressos on their way to the studio.

I really, really, resent these people. I resent their gas-guzzling SUVs, and their $1,200 handbags, and their total lack of interest in *me*! I want neighbors who welcome personal contact. I want to feel that I'm a member of a community. Is that asking too much? If so, so be it.

My dream of a neighborly neighborhood caused me to become addicted to a TV show called *Army Wives*, where a bunch of women on an Army post help each other through their various domestic calamities. God, I loved that show! I found it so reassuring, and it led me to a loco fantasy that I, Annie Korzen, might find happiness living on a military base.

The other day, I ran into Tillie at the post office. "John and I are splitting up," she said. "He has too many women. How are you and Benni getting along? We always used to hear the two of you bickering." Huh? It had never occurred to me that if her voice carried from her house to mine, then the reverse was also true. We hugged goodbye, and Tillie said that she missed me, and she wished we were still neighbors. I said I felt the same way, which, to my utter astonishment, was the truth.

> I hate getting presents. I feel guilty about all that climate-wrecking gift paper. I feel stupid pretending to like things that I have no use for. "Oh goody! A vegan cookbook!" I resent having to keep stuff on the off chance that the gift-giver might drop by and wonder what happened to their Mickey Mouse flowerpot. I know those folks mean well, but I'd so much rather get a dinner invitation!

A Rush to Judgment

At a traditional dinner party, you're supposed to seat people alternately: man, woman, man, woman, and so on. Not me. I have women (and gay men) at one end of the table, and guys on the other. Guess which end is more fun? I have nothing against men (that is *such* a lie!)—I just don't always find them to be the most sparkling conversationalists. That's why I'd rather watch Samantha Bee than some dude on CNN.

I don't have much family, and my girlfriends have been my lifeline. They applaud me when I'm up and support me when I'm down. They are the people I spend holidays with, they are the ones who cried at my son's wedding, and they are the ones who will speak at my funeral—which I plan to attend, by the way. (More about that later.)

The women in my life are so important to me that I was devastated when our friend Charlie got married late in life to a lady named Pamela. She was an aging, refined, gentle Gentile from a small town in Ohio who had old-fashioned, conservative values and dressed accordingly in navy blazers and pearls. I am none of the above, but I had to make nice, because I loved Charlie. I have been through this too many times; in case you haven't noticed, interesting men tend to marry dull women. But Pam was a special challenge.

For starters, how could I possibly be friends with a person who hated garlic? Even worse, she complained to me about a dinner party in Beverly Hills where the hostess had offered my dream menu: three different kinds of pasta. "She served noodles! How cheap is that?" Then one day, she said, "So Annie, tell me, do you by any chance know anyone who's ever tried marijuana?" That confirmed my suspicion that Pam and I lived on different planets.

But over time, I began to realize that she did have some useful qualities. Pam was a college professor of film history, women's studies, and the Great Books. Plus, she wrote historical novels. In other words, she knew everything about everything—the Greeks, Einstein, Shakespeare, and Charlie Chaplin.

This was very convenient for someone like me, who knows nothin' about nothin'—and she allowed me to use her as my personal Wikipedia. When I asked Pam what people ate in the morning in the sixteenth century, she filled me in, at the drop of a hat, on all the details of the bread, cheese, mutton, and ale breakfasts (which sounded a helluva lot tastier than the slimy green Jell-O mold she was serving at that moment).

Then I thought that—just to be courteous—I really ought to read one of her novels. I chose *The Shield of Three Lions*, which is about Richard the Lionheart and the Crusades. What was I thinking? My idea of a good book is a story about a woman who is dealing with a cheating husband while trying to solve a murder, so I was really not looking forward to five hundred pages of "God's feet! T'was wonderous indeed!"

Well, I got the shock of my life. The book was so bloody, so bawdy, so scatological! I couldn't believe that it had been written by Mrs. Prim and Proper! Clearly, I had been too quick to judge her because clearly, a person who writes so enthusiastically about pissing and farting and fucking is a person worth knowing. And that's how it came to pass that Pam and I became best friends.

We talked a few times a week—about books, movies, family, but I always dreaded her inevitable question: "So Annie, tell me, what are you working on?" This drove me nuts, because I had a secret shame, which was that I was never really working on anything. I had always suspected that I might be smart and funny, but I had never figured how to be more than a depressed, mostly unemployed actress and a lively dinner guest. Pam seemed to expect more of me. So, one day, at the ripe old age of blabiddyblahblah, I started looking around for something to do.

I thought maybe I should try my own hand at writing. But what should I write about? There's only one subject that truly fascinates me: *me*! So I started out with some personal stories, and Pam encouraged me to turn them into a show. I called it *Yenta Unplugged.* It took a long time to explain those two words to Pam, but she urged me on. I performed early versions in her Sunset Boulevard living room, and when the show got produced, Pam was the first investor. I returned the favor by causing her to lose every penny.

Then I published some magazine articles and a book and created two more shows. I would not call myself a great success—and I've got the bank account to prove it—but Pam gave me the gift of a vocation. Plus, I discovered that her conservative, old-fashioned values of discipline, diligence, and productivity were a cheap cure for depression.

Pam passed away a while back. It was not a tragic ending; she was in her nineties and had lived a full and fulfilling life. Which is all well and good for her, but what about *me*? I miss her! Let me say this about death: not a fan.

At the memorial service, speaker after speaker described how Pam had taught them, encouraged them, and inspired them. I found these people extremely irritating. I preferred to think that I was the only one who got her special attention. I guess kind and generous people are kind and generous to everyone—but it was still annoying.

When it was my turn, I told how toward the end of her life, Pam was often too frail to speak, so during our visits I would have to do all the talking. No problem; that's my favorite kind of conversation. One day, I went for what I knew would be our last visit—our final chance to connect, our farewell get-together. And by some miracle, the fog lifted. Pam was once again alert and responsive, and we chatted together just like in the old days. During that brief flash of clarity, there came that inevitable moment when she asked, "So Annie, tell me, what are you working on?" And this time—thanks to her—I had an answer.

I discuss '60s rock groups with the letter carrier, I compare detective novels with the librarian, and I suggest acting classes to the waitress at my favorite restaurant. These people are not technically my friends, but I figure any sociable human contact enriches my life. Am I right? Of course I'm right.

Friends with Benefits

You may have already guessed that politically, I'm somewhere to the left of Sean Penn. I think everything should be legal and everything should be free. But I once hung out with some very rich Republicans. That was back when I was a single woman in New York and my piano teacher used to invite his more advanced students for little musical soirées.

One of the students was Peggy Rockefeller, and she often brought her husband, David, the chairman of Chase Manhattan Bank and owner of half the world. The dilemma for me with the Rockefellers was: how do you behave in the presence of such enormous wealth and power? I decided to just be myself, which, in my case, is always a poor choice. Peggy came without David one night, and at the end of the evening, I said, "Peggy, I'm going crosstown. Do you wanna split a cab?" Was I brain-dead? You do not ask a Rockefeller if she wants to split a cab. At first, she had no idea what I was talking about. She finally got it and said, "I have a car waiting. Why don't I just drop you off?"

You see, rich people do not use money. I once watched a TV documentary about the royal family. They were trying to make them look like just ordinary next-door folks, so the camera followed the queen into a sweet shop. (The Brits are very big on sweets because they have no edible food.) The queen got a bag of sugar goodies, and the shop owner said, "That'll be three and tuppence, please."

And the queen had this look of total panic on her face. She had obviously never seen a tuppence in her life, and why should she? She was the Queen of England! What the fuck did she need a tuppence for? She rummaged around in her purse, picked out a coin, and studied it. You could see her thinking, "Oh! How nice! It's *me*!"

Families like the Rockefellers are *our* royalty, and the winter that I hung out with them was a bitterly cold one. I went to a thrift shop and scored a full-length vintage raccoon coat for thirty-five bucks. It was toasty warm, like wearing an electric blanket, and I loved it. (I would not wear fur now, but this was back in the olden times before puffer jackets.) There were, however, two drawbacks. First, it weighed a ton, so when I put it on, I was forced to walk hunched over like Quasimodo. Plus, it had a musty, gamey odor. I figured I would wear it only outdoors, and maybe the stench would give me some space on the subway.

One night, when I went to a piano recital at Lincoln Center, I bumped into Peggy and David and several other members of their family. Peggy said, "Annie, come sit with us, we have some extra seats." They put me on the aisle, and Peggy down at the other end. She noticed my awkwardly huge garment. "Annie, why don't you pass your coat down and we'll put it on an empty seat." Uh-oh. I didn't think it was a good idea, but I didn't know how to refuse. So, I lifted a hundred pounds of stinky raccoon fur and got it hauled down, one at a time, by half a dozen members of the stately Rockefeller family. Not my finest hour.

Ex-Friends

I would like everyone in the world to love me unconditionally. Much to my amazement, this has not happened. There were a few individuals who dropped me because I said something they didn't like. I don't get that. If I dropped people for that reason, I wouldn't have any friends, because everyone's always saying something I don't like. When they do, I have two choices.

A. I say, "Hey, you just said something I don't like." Then we talk about it and resolve the problem, hopefully by them agreeing that I was right.

B. I remind myself of all the other things I like about this person and decide to overlook this one moment of sucky behavior.

What I don't understand are those who walk away forever. Besties who no longer speak. Brothers who have no contact. I'm not saying you should stay in an abusive relationship but, for the most part, so many of these conflicts are dumb and petty and not worth the loss of a human connection. Just listen to Barbra and be a person who needs people.

I was annoyed with a guy I'd known forever because I felt he had been neglectful, and I decided to cross him off my list. Then a close friend died, which reminded me that the herd was thinning, so I got in touch with Mr. Neglectful. He was thrilled to hear from me and invited us for lunch. He and his partner prepared a sumptuous feast, and we spent a great afternoon swapping reminiscences about the old days doing improvisational street theater in New York, where I had played an aging hooker named Dusty Pussy. It was so much more fun than sitting at home and being angry. Hello, *anything* is more fun than sitting at home and being angry. So, if you need some cheering up, make a friendly call to someone who doesn't know you're mad at them. Chances are, you'll feel a lot better. And if you're lucky, you might even get a free meal out of it.

Is there anything more painful than having someone tell you the nasty things that people are saying about you behind your back?

Friends with Stupid Beliefs

I know some folks who have what I consider to be zero-IQ opinions on politics, religion, and modern medicine. Much to my bewilderment, they seem to have the same low opinion of my beliefs. So why, you ask, would I have anything to do with these yo-yos? The answer is that, besides being cuckoo in certain areas, they also happen to be kind, generous, and loyal people. We know we are never going to change each other's minds, so we just avoid those sensitive subjects. Needless to say, our get-togethers tend to be infrequent, and very brief.

Friends from Work

Many of the nail salons in L.A. are owned by Vietnamese refugees, and I'm always fascinated by the warm camaraderie between the owners and the workers. They carpool to work from distant neighborhoods, then they gossip and chatter and giggle all day long. The workers at one shop go to a Korean spa one night a week, and once a year they all take a vacation together—with kids and spouses. Last year it was a cruise; next they're planning a trip to Hawaii. They explained to me, "We are not related, but we love each other like family." Wow! What a blessing to have a job that brings you together with people you adore.

Not everyone is that lucky, however, and I don't know how the unlucky ones do it. I don't know how they spend most of their living hours in the company of—or, even worse, under the supervision of—sexist, racist, humorless, arrogant, asswipes. Which is why I've never had a real job. As a matter of fact, I'm so terrified of being stuck with the wrong people that I created solo performance pieces for myself. That way, if I have a problem with a cast member, I can just tell myself to fuck off.

Friends You Don't Have

Loneliness is a bad thing. It's so bad that it is a major public health concern. There are two kinds of loneliness, and I've experienced both of them. The first, and more painful, kind is a total absence of friends. Maybe you've moved to a new place where you don't know anyone. Maybe you've gone off to college and have always been shy about meeting new people. Maybe you're recently divorced and your friends have abandoned you in favor of your dickhead ex. I have a simple, three-word solution to all these painful scenarios: join a club. Or, better yet, join a few clubs—a book club, a political club, a church club, a pickleball club, a hiking club, a tree-planting club, a bagel-baking club, a Hungarian folk-dancing club. Whatever. There is a club for just about any interest, including the British Lawnmower Racing Association. There's probably even a club called Divorcees Whose Friends Have Abandoned Them for Their Dickhead Exes.

The second kind of loneliness is felt by people who have a partner and plenty of friends, but who still crave a busier social life. Benni could happily stay home every day of the year, including holidays, but I become Maureen Morose if we have a weekend without any plans. When our son, Jonathan, was single, I noticed that his weekend schedule was always something like, "Friday is poker, Saturday I'm having dinner with some college buddies in Little India, and Sunday is Ultimate Frisbee in Central Park." I asked how he always managed to have such a full calendar. "That's easy," he said. "I start making calls on

Thursday." Wha? Call people? That's genius! Why didn't I think of that?

Right now, I don't need an active social schedule because I'm writing this book, and am happy to join Benni in uninterrupted solitude. As a matter of fact, I resent any activity that requires me to get out of my pajamas. But when the book is published, I will definitely pick up that phone every Thursday.

3

MOMMYHOOD

Why hasn't this job been unionized?

Work-Life Balance: There Ain't No Such Thing

> I read somewhere that whatever you don't give a child—those little things like love, compassion, and respect—they will have a hard time giving to others. Fact!

I asked my Danish sister-in-law what it's like to be a working mother in Denmark. After a paid one-year maternity leave, free childcare is available every day until five o'clock. Since the standard workweek in Denmark is thirty-seven hours, it's no problem to pick up your kid at the end of the day. Easy-squeezy, just like here in the States—*not!*

If you have a serious career in this country, thirty-seven hours would be considered a part-time job. Daycare costs a fortune, domestic help costs a fortune, and husbands are too busy with their own sixty-hour work week to be of much help. The best solution for a working mom is to have a retired grandma who lives next door. But these days, grandmas are often still employed, or they are busy with their Zumba classes, or are on a hiking trip with ElderTreks.

Whoever told women "You can have it all!" was a lying liar. You cannot be the world's greatest mom and the world's greatest fighter pilot at the same time. Pick one. And if you pick your career, the good news is that if your kids know that you love them to the moon and back, they will forgive you—eventually—for not being in the kitchen baking brownies when they get home from school. And those women who do choose to be full-time moms are doing one of the world's hardest, and least respected, jobs. My OB-GYN had twins, so she cut back on her office hours. One day, she was dealing with the usual domestic chaos of kids, pets, noise, and mess, when she got called in for an emergency surgery. "My mom came to babysit," she said, "and I got to have a nice, peaceful, hour in the O.R. where I could finally relax a little."

I saw a teenage boy at the beach wearing a shirt that said, "Shut Up, Bitch!" And I wondered about his mother. "Okay, puddin', rise and shine. We're visiting granny today, so which shirt do you want to wear? 'Blow Me,' 'Bite Me,' or 'Up Yours'?"

Singing the Postpartum Blues

I did not have a mother who taught me much about how to function in the world, because she herself didn't know much about how to function in the world. She had escaped the old country, where she didn't fit in, to make a life in the new country—where she also didn't fit in. Like all outcasts, she loved the movies—as did I—and that's where I learned how to function in the world.

When I got pregnant, I knew exactly what to expect—not just from films, but also from all the 1960s feminist dogmas about childbirth. First and foremost, it has to be "natural." No drugs, no episiotomy, no C-sections, no induced labor. If you do any of those things, your child will have lower intelligence, learning disabilities, or seizures, and it will be your fault because poor little you couldn't handle the most excruciating pain that Satan ever devised. Here's the real truth about the "miracle of childbirth"—it's a miracle that anyone who's been through it is willing to do it again.

When I gave birth to my son, the labor went on for too long. I couldn't push him out, so I had to be put under for a forceps delivery. I failed at natural childbirth, and my baby will probably go through life with a dented head.

I'm a single child from a small family, so I had never seen or held a newborn baby before. In films, the mother and child always bond immediately. She gazes upon him with tears of joy and says, "Well, hello there, you beautiful boy." Well, I also gazed upon my son with tears. Tears of profound and hopeless terror. I thought, "Who is this creature, and how the hell am I supposed to keep him alive?"

For starters, I couldn't breastfeed. The baby wasn't latching on properly, and he wasn't getting enough milk because—clearly—I was doing something wrong. So, we switched to formula. And again—according to the birth Nazis—breastfeeding is a sacred, health-giving ritual; feeding your baby formula is child abuse. I had now probably given my poor little dented-headed son an incurable autoimmune disease. I was the worst mother who ever lived.

Benni was working in Denmark at the time, so I gave birth in a foreign country. Big mistake. After the birth, we moved into my father-in-law's country house because—again, from the movies—I fantasized about strolling in beautiful nature with my laughing baby. Well, the house was cramped and uncomfortable, the weather was windy and rainy—it is Denmark, after all—and anyway there was no strolling possible because I was too overwhelmed to figure out how to get dressed in the morning. Plus, I couldn't stop crying.

Now, if you happen to be planning a nervous breakdown, I have a piece of advice for you. Do *not* have it in Denmark. That's because the Danes—like the Brits—consider strong emotions to be bad manners. Danish women are capable, stoic, and independent. I, on the other hand, was fragile, frightened, and exhausted.

I clearly needed some professional help, so Benni managed to make an appointment with a Jewish therapist, thinking that there would be some kind of cultural connection. I talked to the guy for a few minutes, and then he said, "What are all these foolish tears about? Go home, light the Shabbos candles, and start preparing for Rosh Hashanah." Huh? I'd never done any of that stuff. Why was he talking to me like I was a character in *Fiddler on the Roof?*

And then he repeated what everyone had been saying. "Motherhood is instinctive. Nature will show you what to do." Well, when Nature showed me what to do, I must have slept through the class. I kept crying, and Tevye the Shrink said, "I think maybe you need to be hospitalized." Benni arranged for his mother to take the baby, and off we went to the loony bin.

At that point, I knew that I would never be happy again. I would never get better, I would spend the rest of my days in a mental institution in a foreign country, and my darling Benni would live the lonely life of a single dad until he finally connected with the kind of capable, stoic, and independent woman he should have married in the first place. I used to have a nice life, and now I'd lost it all.

The psych ward was in a gloomy old Dickensian hospital in Copenhagen. None of the other patients talked to me—partly because of the language barrier and partly because Danes do not speak to strangers. All the other inmates bathed themselves every day. They rinsed out their underwear in the sink, made their beds neatly, and changed the water in their flower vases while I lay there, unwashed, in my rumpled sheets and sucked on Marlboros while the flowers on my bedside table withered and died from neglect. Not only was I a failure at being a mother, but I was also a failure at being a patient in an insane asylum.

Benni visited every day. No matter how despondent I was, he never let go of his belief that this postpartum depression was a slight temporary glitch in our lives that would soon be over. Poor guy! I was the mental patient, but he was clearly the crazy one.

I wasn't improving, and one day Benni said, "You know something? I'm not sure this is the right place for you."

"Ya think?"

So, we flew back to New York and I was admitted to the psychiatric unit at Mt. Sinai Hospital. My roommate was a novelist who had been married to a famous theater critic. Another patient was a gay guy who was obsessed with Judy Garland movies. Finally! My kind of people!

In group therapy, we were encouraged to share whatever was on our minds, so I asked if anyone knew the most painless and efficient way to kill yourself. I mean, even though I was a teeny tiny bit better, I still wanted a backup plan. Apparently, the other inmates had also given some thought to this subject, and they all offered really cool suggestions. It was the most fun I'd had in months, but the shrink soon put a stop to the discussion. For some strange reason, she felt my topic was "countertherapeutic."

But somehow, wonder of wonders, I started to improve— mostly because the stupid fucking hormonal changes caused by the pregnancy had begun to subside and I was starting to feel like myself again.

One night, some old friends dropped by who entertained me with hilarious stories of their messy lives. The companionship and the laughter suddenly made me feel that maybe life was worth living after all.

The next day Benni brought baby Jonathan for a visit. He was almost four months old, and it was the first time I had seen him since my incarceration. And guess what? That scrawny little newborn creature had grown into a stunningly gorgeous baby. I cautiously picked him up and—wonder of wonders—he smiled at me. Then, just like in the movies, I gazed at him with tears of joy and said, "Well, hello there, you beautiful boy." I was ready to go home.

Jewish Family Services sent a domestic helper, Olga, for two weeks and I finally got the care and guidance and instruction I should have had in the beginning. As Olga showed me how to bathe my son, she urged me on: "You are doing well. You will be a wonderful mother." So, you see, I never really needed hospitalization, drugs, or therapy. All I needed was a *servant*. I am fully aware that I am not Lady Mary on *Downton Abbey*. But lemme tell ya something: *every new mother should be made to feel that she is!*

I never told Jono about any of this, but when he was eighteen, my demented mother-in-law accidentally spilled the beans. I tried to explain: "It was a hormonal imbalance; it wasn't because I didn't love you, blabbedy blah blah…"

And he went, "Hello, why are you making such a big deal about this? I've always known you're a nutcase. What's for dinner?"

So, I started out with absolutely no talent for motherhood, just a blind belief in the movies and a blind belief in the "rules." And despite all those birthing and nursing rules I broke, and despite my bearing zero resemblance to those movie mothers who fall in love with their babies at first sight, Jonathan turned into a smart and healthy and *perfect* man who treats me with more love than I deserve. Everyone always says, "You have such a great kid, and the two of you are so close. How did you do that?" And I laugh to myself: *little do they know*.

Bringing Up Baby: Now and Then

Victorian parents never kissed or hugged their children; they shook hands in the morning. Parenting styles change in every generation, and it can be a challenge for grandparents to adjust to the new norms. Here's how I did things, compared to current fashions.

Early Childhood Activities

> *Now*: Swim classes at six months, singing and signing at nine months, training with a cognitive development coach at one year.

> *Then*: Eating, drinking, pooping, and puking, often simultaneously.

Baby Food

Now: Fat-free, carb-free, gluten-free, locally grown organic produce, electrolyte-free water, grated raw grass-fed liver.

Then: Whatever's in the fridge that could be easily mashed, including last night's spicy meatballs.

Hygiene

Now: No one can touch the baby without first washing their hands, scrubbing with a sanitizer, then donning surgical gloves. The air is filtered, the water is filtered, and all furniture is scrubbed down daily with a nontoxic biodegradable cleaning solution that costs fifty dollars an ounce.

Then: The baby could snack on food that had fallen onto the floor, as long as it hadn't been lying there for more than a day.

Clothing

Now: The standard Baby Gap onesies, tees, and overalls—unless you are French, in which case the kids are more fashionable than you can ever hope to be.

Then: Hand-me-downs from friends and family. The condition wasn't always pristine, but kids don't seem to bothered by the occasional rip or stain, and the price was right.

Babysitters

Now: Nanny cams are installed in every room. In addition to extensive background checks and personal interviews, the applicant's fingerprints must be cleared with Homeland Security.

Then: Hired the high school dropout teenager who lived next door. It was a little disturbing to come back to a house smelling of weed, but the baby was always in a very cheerful mood.

Getting Around

Now: Child must be accompanied by a responsible adult at all times, until he is accompanied down the aisle on his wedding day.

Then: We gave Jono a NYC subway map when he turned twelve, and rarely saw him again until high school graduation.

Screen Time

Now: No screens allowed before age two, and then limited to one or two hours per day of carefully curated programming.

Then: Unlimited access to anything on TV— the world's cheapest babysitter.

After-School Activities

Now: Soccer, tennis, religious instruction, Little League, skateboarding, taekwondo, pottery, circus arts, glee club, pastry-making, software design, karate, indoor rock climbing, animal husbandry, woodworking, and ballroom dancing. And that's just on Mondays.

Then: A couple of piano lessons that led nowhere. This healthy absence of structured activity often led to spontaneous creative pursuits, like leaning out of our apartment window and dropping yogurt onto the heads of passersby.

Entertaining

Now: Children join the guests at the dinner table, and the entire conversation is with and about them.

Then: There was a separate table for the kids, who were told not to interrupt the grown-up chatter. They were, however, close enough to the booze, dirty jokes, and cigarette smoke to feel that they were part of the festivities. It was an excellent lesson in learning how to socialize.

Character Building

Now: When he wants to know why he can't eat all his Halloween candy in one sitting, you gently and lovingly explain the consequences of that action until he understands and accepts your point of view.

Then: When he wanted to know why he couldn't eat all his Halloween candy in one sitting, you shouted at the top of your lungs, "Because I say so, and I'm the mother!" Then you'd grab the candy and eat it all in one sitting.

Discipline

Now: After a five-minute timeout for bad behavior, be sure to tell him that you love him, even though you're a wee bit disappointed that he stabbed the cat.

Then: Grounded him for a month, expressed your regrets about having had children, and shared your fervent hope that one day his kids would cause him the same misery he was causing you.

Choosing a School

Now: Research test scores, student-teacher ratios, ergonomic chairs, and snack quality. Find out how diverse the student population is. It may be too little or too much, depending on where you stand on diversity.

Then: The nearest public school. The curriculum was limited, but a library card was an affordable supplement. When our son complained that the teachers were boring, we gave him our standard answer to any complaint: "Just suck it up." We went on to explain that school was *supposed* to be boring; that's why it's called "school" and not House of Fun.

Birthday Parties

Now: Magicians, jungle animals, sushi bars, solar-powered bounce houses, trampoline classes with circus acrobats, gift bags from Tiffany and Apple.

Then: McDonald's takeout, followed by card games played for money where the grown-ups always won—with many admonitions of, "Hey, buddy! There's no crying in blackjack!"

Rights of Passage

Now: Destination bar mitzvahs in exotic lands like Hawaii, Tahiti, or St. Barts, where the grown-ups eat too much and the kids misbehave like the stupid adolescents that they are.

Then: Destination bar mitzvahs in exotic lands like the Bronx, Brooklyn, Queens, or Riverdale, where the grown-ups ate too much and the kids misbehaved like the stupid adolescents that they were.

Summer Vacations

Now: Fat camp, music camp, tech camp, joining parents on a luxury African safari.

Then: A free one-week stay in the country at the home of elderly relatives whose idea of a fun-filled evening was listening to local farming news on the radio before lights out at eight thirty p.m.

The Teen Years

Now: The whole family should see a therapist twice weekly to prevent the pitfalls of drug addiction, careless sexual activity, and eating disorders.

Then: All teenagers were known to be dangerous sociopaths, so the safest thing to do was to have as little contact with them as possible. If they managed to survive those turbulent years in one piece, we congratulated ourselves on a job well done.

"Boomerang" Kids

Now: After college, the child moves back home while supposedly looking for a job. He spends the next decade getting high, playing video games, and occasionally removing his socks from the kitchen table.

Then: "Boomerang kids"? What's that?

In conclusion, the most important thing to remember about child-rearing is that whatever choice you make, your kid will resent you for it. So you might as well just do what's most comfortable for you.

Why Worry? Because That's Your Job

I was raised by a woman who could have won an Olympic Gold in Jewish mothering. She made me wear galoshes on sunny days ("It might rain, you never know!"); she wouldn't let me leave the house with wet hair ("You'll catch pneumonia!"); and if I was ten minutes late coming home from school, she was ready to display a Missing Persons photo in the post office. The worrying was nonstop, relentless, constant, and all those other words that mean "24/7." "You're going to Manhattan? Be careful! It's not a Jewish neighborhood!" And I swore that when I grew up and had a child of my own, I would not ever be an interfering, overprotective Jewish mother.

I think you can guess what happened next. I had a son. Oy! One day Jono jumped up to throw a stupid basketball, and when he landed, his knee snapped. He couldn't have just played Scrabble? As we entered the emergency room, he warned me, "Now remember it's my knee, so control yourself, okay?" I promised to behave, and as the young resident examined him, I did my best imitation of a calm and collected human female person.

"Yes, Doctor? Ligament reconstruction, surgery, crutches, physical therapy? Okey-dokey, no problemo. Just one teeny-weeny question. Will my son be in any pain?"

Now this resident was a pimply-faced, teenage, bar mitzvah *bocher*, and his answer to me was: "Now, Mrs. Korzen, let's not be a Jewish mother!"

I did not take kindly to this snide remark from Doogie Howser in a yarmulke, so I asked him the most important question: "Excuse me, Doctor, but where exactly did you go to medical school? ...Barbados? I don't think so. Let's bring down the chief of surgery, shall we?" Jono turned red with embarrassment, but I figured better red than dead.

Then I read this novel, *The Joy Luck Club*, about American-born daughters and their immigrant Chinese mothers who force them to take piano lessons and compete in chess tournaments. And I thought, "Those Chinese mothers are very familiar." And I saw this movie *My Left Foot*. Everyone believes this kid is brain-damaged, except his mother. She's right; he turns out to be a genius. And I thought, "That Irish mother is very familiar."

Then a Black girlfriend called about her teenage son. His self-esteem had taken a dive because he couldn't find a summer job, so she asked me to hire him for some tech help. "I will pay his salary. Just don't tell him where the money's coming from," she told me. It sounded very familiar indeed.

So, how do you like that? I may have turned into my mother, but it seems I'm not the only one. And maybe that's not such a bad thing after all.

The Too-Jewish Wedding

Being a parent is a Catch-22. Your main job is to prepare your kids to separate from you, while your main instinct is to keep them as close to you as possible. Every time Jonathan left for school, for camp, for college—actually, every time he left the house—I felt a heartbreaking sense of loss.

After an extended bachelorhood, Jono finally called with the dreaded news: he and his longtime girlfriend, Alisa, were engaged. I now had to face the fact that I would no longer be the leading lady in his life. It sucked, but I'd heard there was a chance that I might die someday, so it was good to know that my son wouldn't be alone. Then he told me about the wedding plans: a huge, formal affair in New York (we had already moved to L.A.) that would be based on old-school Jewish customs.

I went, "Oooh, that sounds wonderful!" I hung up, poured a glass of wine, and spent the rest of the day wailing on the phone with the Yenta Brigade.

"Have they lost their minds? It's too big, it's too formal, and it's too Jewish…. What do you mean 'It's not my wedding'? Why does everyone keep saying that?" They all assured me that everything would work out and I should just relax and enjoy it. What was wrong with these women? They ought to know that *nothing* makes me more anxious than being told to relax.

I forced myself to say nothing to Jono about those crazy-ass wedding plans. For starters, what was that black-tie requirement? In our artsy/hippie/boho crowd, we did not party in tuxes and evening gowns. And why was there such a huge guest list? People were not going to fly in from all over the world for a glass of champagne and some chopped liver.

Plus, I was not comfortable with all this traditional Jewy stuff that Alisa had been brought up with: a rabbi saying prayers, a custom-designed Hebrew marriage contract, and one hundred baby blue yarmulkes ordered from UnderTheChuppah. com. Our family is not observant in any way. We are secular

Jews who believe in the time-honored ancestral values of eating out, bargain-shopping, and arguing about whether the room is too hot or too cold. But once again, I keep silent.

Things started to get frantic. I had to buy a gown, we had to fly to New York, and Benni's huge Danish family was coming in from Copenhagen. We would take them for a Chinese dinner as an introduction to Jewish-American culture. And then things went from frantic to *insane*: Benni's cousin was coming with his two ex-wives, and they were all staying in the same room with one king-sized bed. And now you know how the Danes got to be the happiest people in the world.

I went to a wardrobe sale at a TV studio and found a beaded gown that still had a $1,200 price tag on it. I paid twenty bucks—and kept the tag in case I wanted to resell it on eBay. Benni dug out his old tux from 1967, which still fit perfectly, as long as he didn't button it or zip up the fly.

Much to my surprise, people actually did fly into Manhattan from all over the world, and I have to admit that everyone looked fantabulous in their elegant evening clothes. And then a weird thing happened: I got a little shiver when Benni's very assimilated half-Jewish half-Lutheran Danish family put yarmulkes on their heads for the first time in their lives.

The ceremony began with four young men carrying the wedding canopy down to the front of the room. The canopy was very simply draped with Alisa's late father's prayer shawl. Once again, I got a little shiver at this ancient ritual. What was going on with me?

The music changed, and Alisa, the radiant bride, entered. And when my son looked at her, I felt that same heartbreaking sense of loss that I used to feel when he went off to school, to camp, to college. Only this time, I knew he wasn't coming back. He was marrying her…and divorcing me.

Jonathan broke the glass, and everyone yelled, "*Mazel tov!*" We danced back up the aisle to those driving klezmer rhythms, and we kept dancing, clapping, eating, drinking, laughing, and crying the whole night long. All the things I had worried about—the formal attire, the big crowd, the Jewy stuff—turned out to be all the things I loved most about the wedding. I am so glad that I did the most important—and difficult—thing a mother can do: I kept my big mouth shut!

The Reluctant Grandmother

My Danish mother-in-law, Mia, was a lunatic who drove everybody crazy, but I loved her because she had the soul of an artist. When Mia wasn't playing music, she was painting. And when she wasn't painting, she was knitting. And when she wasn't knitting, she was a lunatic who drove everybody crazy. Jonathan grew up wearing Mia's colorful homemade scarves and hats and blankets. When he outgrew them, I packed them all into a box for the children I assumed he would have one day.

What children? Jonathan and Alisa were forty when they got married and did not seem to be on the baby track, which was fine with me. I gave away the box of scarves and hats and blankets without much grief. Unlike the clichéd Jewish mother, I never really yearned to be a grandparent. I don't much care for children (or anything else that pulls focus away from me). They're demanding and raucous and—let's be honest here—*bo*-ring. You can't have a serious adult conversation with them until they're—well—serious adults. But for some bizarre reason,

Jono and Alisa love kids, and not having a family would have left a big gaping hole in their lives.

They were late starters, so they decided to try for a domestic adoption, which was a costly journey into the world of frustration, disappointment, and heartbreak. There was the chain-smoking mother who refused to have any prenatal care. There was the overweight food blogger who didn't realize she was pregnant until she went to the hospital with stomach pains and delivered a baby after nine months of daily wine tastings. There was the teenager who answered a Craigslist ad but turned out to be a lonely, attention-seeking virgin.

At long last, they were offered a healthy little girl from a normal-seeming woman, and it looked like a done deal. I was loading up on pink onesies at Ross Dress for Less until—at the very last minute—the adoption agency said, "Sorry, this is not going to work out. The mother forgot to tell us that she wants young, Christian parents with a stay-at-home mom."

Then one day, things got real. An attractive, intelligent woman who loved her son but couldn't keep him had the good sense to choose Jono and Alisa to be his parents. And even though I am not a baby-lover, and even though I had zero desire to be a grandmother, I can tell you, with total impartiality, that this chubby, smiling, dimpled little boy is the best, the brightest, and the most beautiful child in the history of the world. Oh, and one more thing: he's Black.

It turns out that 70 percent of Jewish adoptive families take in children of color. They would probably prefer a Jewish child, but Jews do not give away their unwanted babies; they keep them so that they can remind them daily of the great sacrifice they made.

Now, the way I express love for someone is by worrying about them. And I have lots of reasons to worry about the safety of my grandson. So, here's my plan: he will wear glasses even if he doesn't need them, and carry a violin even if he doesn't play one. Because he's big and he's dark, and stupid people will feel threatened by him.

Stupid people like me. I was walking alone on a dark empty street, and I saw a tall young Black man walking toward me. My heart started racing as I wondered if I was in danger. As he passed me with a polite nod, there was that shameful moment in which I knew that he knew that I had been afraid. And I've experienced that shameful moment many times in my life, because you do not know who a person is just by looking at them.

And now my precious grandson will have to deal with the same garbage. Garbagy stuff is already happening. People say things like, "Aw, look at the cute little Harlem Globetrotter!"

And when some random bigmouth asked, "Why did they want a Black baby?" I said, "They didn't. They wanted a human baby."

I did not add, "So shut your fucking piehole, you dumb twat!" because I am a lady.

The great irony is, my first serious love was a Black guy I went to college with. But if I had married Billy, I would have been part of an interracial family, and who needed that challenge? It's tough enough just dealing with all the Jew crap.

Isn't life strange? I thought I didn't want to be a grandmother, and I thought I didn't want to be part of an interracial family. But when those things actually happened, everything fell into place. So, just like with that Jewish wedding, maybe what we think we want or don't want has very little to do with what really makes us happy. And who knows? As the world keeps evolving, maybe by the time my precious Max grows up, he might be able to walk down a dark street without anyone feeling threatened—or anyone threatening him.

Max and I might look "mismatched" to most people, but most people have a lot to learn. Max and I have the same musicality, the same sense of humor, the same love of words, and the same weird imagination. We are as matched as any kid and his granny could be, and it is a match made in heaven.

Meanwhile, I was doing my annual purge of Benni's closet the other day and came across a beautiful knit scarf that Mia had made for him. I'm giving it to Max, and when he wears it, the chain of our family will be unbroken.

Kids and Cash

Alisa is teaching Max how to handle money. Whenever he gets a cash gift, Max can spend some of it however he wants, has to save some of it, and has to donate some of it to charity. How smart is that?

Another smart mom is my friend Amy Anderson whose daughter, Aubrey, played the adopted child on *Modern Family*. Aubrey has been taught to spend wisely, and Amy has encouraged her to do volunteer work for several local charities. [Applause!]

A trust-fund kid I know put her wedding registry on Target, because she didn't want to oblige her guests to spend a lot of money on fancy gifts. How thoughtful is that? A lot more so than some of those outrageous bougie registries with items like a bamboo sheet set for $360.

But then there are some of my least favorite humanoids: the entitled, bratty spawn of the richie-rich, like the one I encountered at a yard sale in Beverly Hills. Dad was obviously a successful showbiz guy, in the TV producer uniform of vintage rock band T-shirt and backward baseball cap. I was considering a box of books for thirty dollars, because Benni was dabbling in the rare-book business at that time. But I wasn't sure these had any value so, in the customary yard sale bargaining ritual, I asked showbiz Dad if he would take twenty bucks.

His ten-year-old son had the nerve to rebuke me. "That's crazy! What difference does ten dollars make?" Butthead Dad did not admonish him.

I did not say, "How dare you speak to me—or any adult—that way, you spoiled little piece of fuckturd?" because I am a lady. Instead, I left the books and stole a toy on the way out, which I donated to my local thrift store. You may call that theft; I call it social justice.

Teenage Privacy: I Don't Think So

When Jonathan was sixteen, I read his diary. Please do not reproach me for disregarding boundaries and disrespecting my son's privacy. Boundaries? Privacy? For a teenager? You're kidding, right? Teenage boys are mentally deranged creatures who live for sports, violent music, and auto-eroticism. Jono had mood swings, he was secretive, he was quarrelsome, and his room was as grubby as his brain cells. If you asked him a simple question, like, "How was history class today?" he would say, "Fine," accompanied by a lengthy sigh that expressed his total contempt of his imbecile parent.

It was all normal, everyday, obnoxious, teenage behavior, but I needed to make sure that there was nothing more serious going on. Was he being bullied? Was he planning to burn down his school? Was he a member of the Hitler Admiration Society? So, fuck privacy! I went ahead and violated those bulldoody parent-child "boundaries." I read the goddamn diary, and I'm so glad I did. It was a sweet, sensitive account of absolutely nothing to worry about. Jono remained sweet and sensitive, and years later, when I confessed my sin, he once again exhaled a lengthy sigh—expressing not contempt but amusement—and said, "Why am I not surprised? By the way, you're paying for the brunch."

4

WORKING GIRL

Ups and downs—mostly
downs, until one day...

What's Wrong with This Picture?

n 1993, I published an op-ed piece in the *Los Angeles Times* called "Casting with More Chutzpah Might Help." It was about the "whitewashing" of Jewish female characters. The last line was, "If the life of Golda Meir ever gets remade, we should show a little chutzpah and boycott the box office if she's played by Meg Ryan." The biopic of Golda Meir has recently been made—starring Helen Mirren. Golda was previously played by Ingrid Bergman. Some things never change. Jewish men in the entertainment industry rarely cast (or date, or marry) Jewish-looking women. This is bad news for me, because my face has "Shebrew" written all over it.

I once read for a commercial that I knew I would book because I had worked with the director, Stu Lefkowitz, before, and he was looking for an "Annie Korzen type." Holy can-noli, talk about a sure thing! Guess what? I did not get the job. Stu Lefkowitz hired a perky little blonde. I was too Jewish to play *myself*!

My agent submitted my name for a movie, but the director, Harold Shlomansky, wouldn't see me. He said I was too Jewish. Again, I hear that all the time, but it was for the role of a *rabbi*. Harold Shlomansky was seeing only Gentile actresses because, as he put it, he wanted to be sure that the character was likeable.

I'm not saying that you should show proof of Jewishness to play these roles. Valerie Harper was terrific as Rhoda; she had authentic ethnic vibes and was totally believable. But Felicity Jones as Ruth Bader Ginsburg? Michelle Williams as Mrs. Fabelman? And Julianne Moore as Jesse Eisenberg's Jewish mother?

The same Jewface tradition holds on Broadway. Neil Simon and Arthur Miller wrote plays full of Jewish angst and humor, and the actresses all looked and sounded like there had been a sign on the casting session door that said, "No Jewess Need Apply."

In Hollywood, "Jewish-looking" equals "ugly." That's for the women; the guys, as usual, do a lot better. Hence, all those "The Schmuck and the Shiksa" movies, where I always wonder why the classy, beautiful WASP chooses to share her life—let alone her bed—with that insecure, juvenile loser. Surely, she could do better. Then I remember that she's not a real person; she's just the manifestation of the fantasies of the insecure, juve-nile filmmakers.

Do I sound bitter? I am. Do I sound angry? I am. But I'm also something else. I'm sad—the kind of sadness that comes from unrequited love, because I love all those Jewish writers, producers, and directors who disdain women who look and sound like me. Besides being insecure and juvenile, they are also smart, funny, sensitive, and talented, and I would like nothing better than to hang out with them—but they have made it clear that I'm not wanted. I wish I had the self-assurance to say, "Their loss."

Jerry Waved Hello

One day, I got lucky. My agent called with an audition for a few lines on a new sitcom. A better-known actress had turned it down, saying the role was too small for her. In Hollywood, the general rule is, "Don't ever accept a job as a bit player, because then you will be stuck in that category forever." The good news is that there are exceptions to every rule. The bad news is: not in my particular case. But self-respect was not a luxury I could afford, so I went in and got the job.

To get to the shoot, I was confronted with one of my top ten phobias: driving a car. To me, the automobile is a weapon of mass destruction. I use only surface streets, I avoid left turns, and I do not *merge*. I carefully planned my route to the set in Burbank, but my addled brain missed the turnoff to Cahuenga Boulevard, and I suddenly found myself in the fast lane of the Hollywood Freeway, going at my top speed of thirty-two miles an hour. To get to the approaching exit, I had to cross five lanes of rush-hour traffic. By some miracle, I survived and got to do yet another paltry little bit part, but this one changed my life.

When the show aired, Benni didn't get it. "It's not about anything," he said. How right he was. The show was *Seinfeld*. My few lines turned into the recurring character of Doris

Klompus in the Florida condo. My husband, Jack Klompus, was always fighting with Jerry's father, so I was in some of the classic episodes: "The Pen," "The Cadillac," "Raincoats." My role was so trifling that the audience didn't even notice when I played a second character: the obnoxious lady sitting next to Elaine on an airplane. (Because of my looks, obnoxious characters are my specialty.)

Now, when you walk onto a TV set as a bit player, your job is to hit your mark, say your lines, and not make waves. At lunch, the principals sit together, and you do not join their table unless you're invited. If they are in the chair next to you in makeup, you do not speak unless you are spoken to. You are the *outsider*, the interloper who has crashed the party. This is torture for someone like me, because all I've ever wanted was to be an *insider*.

But since I did several episodes, I did eventually get friendly with the cast, which mostly meant listening to stories about their sex lives, my idea of a good time. Liz Sheridan, who played Jerry's mom, told me about her affair with James Dean. Jason Alexander claimed to be the world's best kisser. And Sandy Baron, who played my husband, shared every salacious detail about the time he'd been set up on a blind date with a woman who actually turned out to be blind. Best sex he ever had.

One of my favorite cast members was Jerry Stiller, who in real life was nothing at all like the nutso Frank Costanza. I once ran into Jerry at a Chekhov play, and he awed me with a scholarly, erudite analysis of the piece. And then he posed the question that serious thespians have been asking each other since time began, "So? Ya workin'?"

The sad truth was that I was still a mostly unemployed bit player—until the day I realized that I was a little famous. I was at a party and met one of those *Seinfeld* fanatics who watches every rerun. Not only did he know who both my insignificant characters were, but he could quote all my insignificant lines. Another guest was impressed, even though it was clear that she'd never seen the show. "You were on *Steinfield*? Could I get an autograph for my nephew?" Then I went to Australia to perform one of my solo shows, and the newspaper headline said, "*Seinfeld* actress coming to Sydney!"

We have a friend who is a major Hollywood player. This guy was so uninterested in me that he used to introduce me as an afterthought: "Oh, and this is Benni's wife." One night we were dining with him in a popular Chinese restaurant. I chewed my moo shu in silence while Mr. Hollywood spoke only to Benni.

Then I spotted someone waving at me and calling my name. I went over, and it was Jerry Seinfeld, who—nice guy that he is—just wanted to say hello. Everyone in the restaurant stared, and I could sense them thinking, "Who is that woman schmoozing with Jerry Seinfeld? She must be Somebody." When I returned to our table, Mr. Hollywood actually began to include me in the conversation. He now introduces me as, "And this is my very dear friend Annie Korzen. You've probably seen her on *Seinfeld*."

I sometimes think about the actress who turned down the role because it was too small. True, I had only a few lines in a few episodes. But those residual checks are still trickling in, and over the years, *Seinfeld* has earned me mucho moolah. I smell a moral lesson here, and I think it has to do with the power of always saying, "Yeah, why not?"

I got really lucky, because no one could have possibly predicted this show's global success. After all, the characters are, for the most part, pretty sleazo. They're whiny; they're devious; they're thoughtless narcissists. Why do gazillions of people all over the world want to spend so much time with these losers? Here's my theory: we all want to be accepted for who we are, and that's what Jerry and George and Elaine and Kramer do. No matter what crazy-ass things they say to each other, no matter what crazy-ass things they do to each other, they always just let it go and move on. They forgive and forget—which is how we treat people we love. So, the TV show that's "not about anything," is really about a big fat F-word called family, and I will be forever grateful that I got to be a small part of that adventure. (Larry David would throw up at what I just wrote here.)

Now comes the bad news. At first, I was pretty comfortable with Jerry and Larry, but when the show became a global phenomenon, I got intimidated by their fame. They hadn't really changed, but I became shy and awkward in their presence. When most people get shy and awkward, they get tongue-tied. I have the opposite reaction: my tongue gets *un*tied, and I can't stop chattering. Each time I ran into them, I launched into a crazed, desperate, nonstop, inappropriate monologue, totally ignoring the forced smiles on their faces and the uneasy look in their eyes.

"HiJerryhiLarryhowareyouareyouhavingdinner?Whatare youhaving?Isthatanygood?Who'sthis?Yourgirlfriend?Isshe Jewish?That'snicedoyoucookathome?Whatdoyoumake?Doyou cookeverynight?Yadayadayada."

My brain would yell at me, "Shut your stupid piehole, you are making a gigantic ass of yourself!" but my mouth paid no attention to my brain and just kept yammering on. Is there a medication for verbal diarrhea?

In Praise of Failure

I didn't start acting until I was in my midthirties, so I've had a lot of catching up to do. I've never done Broadway, I've never done Shakespeare, and I'm still hoping that one day I will get to do a nude scene. My biggest dream was to be a regular on a sitcom. There were only three things standing in my way: my looks, my age, and my lack of talent. But the heart wants what it wants. And mostly, what my heart wanted was to feel *important*. And I still want that. I want to hang out with George Clooney at his villa in Italy. I want Tina Fey to call me when she needs a laugh. I want the Dalai Lama to sign up for my storytelling class. In other words, I want everyone I admire to admire me back.

I began by doing the usual variety of crap jobs. Children's theater, where one kid asked, "Are you a puppet?" Free shows in nursing homes where I was in the middle of a song when a resident yelled out, "Hey, is this gonna be over soon? It's almost time for cake!" One line in a soap opera: "The doctor will see you now." And—the very worst of all—tedious, brain-sucking days on the sweltering sidewalks of New York as a movie extra.

During those lean years, I did, however, accomplish one very important task: I wrote and rehearsed my Oscar, Tony, and Emmy award speeches. You know how those prize winners often fumph around at a total loss for words? I don't get that; they have had *all of their lives* to prepare!

Then we moved to L.A. and I began to get semiregular work as a TV actress. I still muddled through endless stretches of unemployment, so I decided to try writing and perform-ing my own words—as a storyteller. Once again, this meant a steady diet of struggle and humiliation. One event was at a grungy barbecue joint deep in the bowels of the San Fernando Valley. When I got there, I discovered that most of the audience spoke English as a second language—the first language being Mongolian. Needless to say, my piece about my son's Jewish wedding did not rock the house.

Another show was on the freezing front patio of a coffeeshop in East Hollywood with fire engines screaming by every few minutes. Six storytellers, with four people in the audience. Everyone was under twenty-five, so once again, my piece about my son's Jewish wedding did not rock the house. Much warmer applause was given to one guy's detailed description of his battle with genital herpes, which he did in rhyming couplets. "I got a great shock / When I looked at my cock."

One ray of light during those dark days was my husband. After each disaster, Benni's response was always the same: "You were terrific."

"What are you talking about? I got zero laughs!"

"That's because they were really listening. Trust me, they loved you."

Just like during my postpartum crisis, Benni had more faith in me than I had myself. And that's what you want in a life partner.

My goal as a storyteller was to appear on The Moth Mainstage. Every time I performed, I sent them a video, saying, "Hi! Here's a new piece. Hope we'll work together soon." I did that several times a year for nine years. They occasionally gave me a few words of encouragement but never booked me. One day, I sent them what I thought was a sensational story and, once again, I got no response. So, I decided to give up. I really felt I belonged there, but I would have to accept the fact that it was just another dream that was not going to come true. I medicated my heartbreak by dragging Benni to an all-you-can-eat Indian buffet. Everyone knows that samosas can cure sadness.

The following week, I got a call from New York. "Hi, Annie, this is Catherine at The Moth. Thanks for being so patient. Listen, we'd like you to perform with us in L.A., Saint Louis, Berkeley, and The Schubert Theater in Boston. We'll also put you on our radio show and on our website, and maybe in our next book. Oh, and the story we want is that wonderful piece about your son's Jewish wedding."

So, just like with the acting, I kept getting nowhere until one day I woke up and found I was somewhere. One day I asked someone at The Moth why it had taken so long for them to book me.

"Oh," she said, "you got better."

Oh my God that I don't believe in! It turns out that constant failure is a terrific learning opp. Some people are overnight successes, and some people, like me, just have to keep flunking out until they finally get a passing grade.

Now, in my third act, I have a whole new and totally unexpected career. Just before the pandemic hit, I was asked to lead a storytelling event in a home for mentally challenged people. I really *really* didn't want to do it but felt morally obliged to accept. That decision to do the right thing changed my life, because I struck up a friendship with one of the other volunteers.

Enter Mackenzie. Mackenzie is a tall, gorgeous, soft-spoken thirty-year-old from a churchgoing family. Again, I am none of the above. But we both like vintage fashion, women writers, and sipping girly cocktails in outdoor cafes, and we soon became best buds. One day, I was telling Mackenzie how I'd like to find a larger audience for my performance pieces, and I was thinking about posting some little clips on Instagram.

"Ugh, Instagram is so toxic," she said. "You should be on TikTok."

"Me? No way! TikTok is about half-naked young girls putting on makeup and shaking their booties."

"Trust me, Annie, you would blow up. I will film the clips and post them for you." This crazy idea turned out to be the most significant "Yeah, why not?" moment of my life.

I've always been criticized for talking too much and for being too candid. On TikTok, I can use the writing and performing skills that I developed during those many years of falling on my ass, and I'm allowed to talk as much and as candidly as I feel like. Much to my amazement, people started listening. All kinds of people. Large numbers of people. From all over the world.

I have been given the title of "grandfluencer." (Mackenzie hates that word, because it mostly applies to women, whereas older men have always been given respect—and political office—but I'll take any title I can get.)

The *L.A. Times* called. *CBS Evening News* called. *Inside Edition* called. Dr. Phil called.

But here's the best thing that happened. I was rehearsing my usual four and a half lines on a film, *Moving On*, when the director, Paul Weitz, took me aside for a moment. Now Paul Weitz cowrote and codirected one of my favorite movies, *About a Boy*, so I am a major fan. And I knew what he was going to say to me, because every director I have ever worked with says the same thing: "Annie, your timing is great. But on the next take could you just…bring it down a little bit?"

But that's not what Paul Weitz said. What he said was, "Annie, I just have to tell you how much I love your story about your grandson on TikTok."

Oh my fucking God! My life-long dream has finally come true! Someone I admire admires me back! And it only took eighty-three years!

Oh…sorry, I have to stop now. The Dalai Lama's calling.

It's hard to get my work done unless I have a fun event to look forward to, and I can't enjoy a fun event unless I've gotten my work done.

5

SACRED AND PROFANE

Jews, Jesus, and halal

Bibles and Brisket

I am very Jewish—whatever that means. By the way, I have a Swedish friend who pronounces it "Yewish," and I think I like that. Anyway, I may have a recognizable Jewish identity, but the fact is, I know jack about Judaism. I do not celebrate the holidays, I do not understand the rituals, I have never belonged to a temple, and the only Hebrew word I know is "*shalom*." In other words, despite how the world labels me, I am not a good Yew.

After the Holocaust, my parents turned away from the old beliefs. My immigrant mother would say, "If there is a God, I don't like Him." My folks were lefty union labor atheist socialists. They belonged to any organization that had a "W" in it: the International Ladies Garment Workers Union, the International Workers Order, and The Workmen's Circle.

On Yom Kippur, while the rest of our Bronx neighborhood was going to shul, Momma and I would sneak downtown to a Broadway musical because—and I say this with Yewish pride—Yom Kippur is the easiest day of the year to get theater tickets. So, we were pariahs: no Passover Seders, no Purim festivals, no nothing.

I brought my son up the same way. But when Jono turned thirteen, we did want him to have some kind of coming-of-age ceremony, so he got lessons in Jewish history. We invited a bunch of people for lunch, and Jonathan read a paper he had written called "Jewish Values in the Modern World." Plus, I had this great idea of asking each guest to give Jono a list of their ten favorite books and ten favorite movies, so that he could grow up with his own personal liberal arts guide. Am I brilliant or what?

This alternative bar mitzvah was a unique and unconventional celebration, and everybody loved it. Everybody—except my son. He hated it. He accused us of being "hippy-dippy cheapos," adding, "Why didn't I have a real bar mitzvah in a real synagogue with a big fancy party afterward? Then I would have gotten lots of checks instead of those stupid lists!" And I reminded him that in our family, going to temple was not on our list of fun things to do.

I have attended services occasionally because—even though I have no interest in God—from time to time I do enjoy being in a room full of Yews. That's what makes us different from other faiths; you can still be Jewish without being a believer. There are many secular Jews; there are no secular Baptists.

I go to shul in the hopes of hearing about large ideas: compassion, tolerance, goodness. But then they always spoil things with those long, repetitive prayers: "Blessedareyou,Lord,ourGod, sovereignoftheuniverse.YouareholyandYourNameisholyand holybeingspraiseYoudailyforalleternity."

And just as you're nodding off, they make you stand up: "Please rise." Why? Why must I rise? I don't wanna rise! I'm wearing heels! I wanna *sit*!

Jonathan is now grown and guided by his more traditional wife. He has become a holiday Jew. He fasts on Yom Kippur (until he gets really hungry), and he dips an apple into honey on the New Year. He lights the Hanukkah menorah. I have failed as a mother; my son married a woman who is not an exact replica of me. But there's a bright side: Jono and Alisa host a seder every year, which I happily attend, because I always honor the Eleventh Commandment, sacred to Jews from time immemorial: "Thou shalt not refuse free food." It's not the Bible that excites me, it's the brisket.

So, when a friend invites me to attend a Bible study group with a rabbi, I go: "Me? Are you high?"

"There's going to be a fabulous catered lunch."

"Okay, I'm in."

And in the middle of a lot of snoozeworthy God-said-this and God-said-that, the rabbi says something that absolutely blows me away: "The most common phrase in the Bible is 'Do not be afraid, for I will be with you.'"

Get out! Fear! That, I can relate to. I live in fear. My middle name is fear! Maybe if I were lucky—or foolish—enough to feel God's presence, I would feel safe in the world. But I am on my own, and will have to find my way all by myself. And I will have to keep creating my own rituals, like that hippy-dippy cheapo secular bar mitzvah.

Jono, on the other hand, will give his son a more conventional ceremony. They will go to temple, they will chant the prayers, and they will cash the checks. And you know something? I'm glad that my son has a sense of belonging that I've never had. It is not easy being an outsider. It is lonely, and you miss out on a lot of parties. And even though I am a devout heathen, I guarantee you that when my little Max is called to the bimah to read from the Torah, I will shed a few tears. As long as I don't have to *rise*!

> "The self-assured believer is a greater sinner in the eyes of God than the troubled disbeliever."
>
> —Søren Kierkegaard
>
> This should be on a T-shirt.

My Night with Baby Jesus

There is a lot I like about Christmas: the mulled wine, the smell of pine leaves, the twinkling lights. Did I mention the mulled wine? There is a lot I don't like about Christmas. I get really sick of those nonstop carols that begin somewhere around Labor Day—especially the yuck versions with drum machines and Vegas stylings. A beautiful hymn like "Silent Night" should not be crooned like a '50s pop single. Also, I'm not sure why you'd observe a religious holiday by stampeding Best Buy on Black Friday. At least Hanukkah has universal significance. I mean, what living human doesn't worship fried food?

Then there's the old JC himself. Christ the Savior. The image is not very joyful—the cross, the nails, the thorns, the blood. But most of what this pinko commie Jew had to say is pretty cool. (Let's face it: with all his talk about peace and compassion and social justice, Jesus was the Bernie Sanders of his day.) My biggest problem with Christmas is simply having to say it: I guess it's a Yewy thing, but the word just sticks in my throat. "Merry Chrma, Morry Kakas, Murr Crssas."

One year, some friends suggested we attend midnight Mass with them. I was curious, so I answered with my usual, "Yeah, why not?" The church looked quite festive with shimmering candles, pine wreaths, and huge red velvet bows. I was wearing a bright red top, like most of the other women, because when you're a fish out of water, you should at least be fashion-appropriate. The ushers were very friendly, which meant a lot more awkward muttering of "Merry Chrma, Merry Kakas, Murr Crssas."

The service started, and there was the usual annoying up-and-down-and-up-again of sitting and standing and, worst of all, kneeling, which was not just annoying but painful as well. There was also way too much incense—nostril-clogging, suffocating clouds of incense.

But I did like the robes, and I did like the music. Most of all, I liked the sense of theater and pageantry and ancient history. And then they walked down the aisle carrying a large doll that represented the infant Jesus, and he was being held high up in the air so everyone could worship him. I thought, "Okay, now I get it! That's what this whole megillah is about! They are celebrating a child! A pure and innocent babe. Forget that nasty crucifix; this is an image I can relate to." I started to be really glad I came.

Then it was time for the sermon. Father Dylan's talk was about kindness. As in, "The world needs much more of it. We must each remember to practice kindness every single day of our lives."

It was not very profound. It was pretty basic stuff, a notion that's as simple and sweet and innocent as a newborn child. But it resonated with me, because I had suspected for a while already that I was not kind enough. The reason I suspected it was because people kept telling me that I was not kind enough. I was judgy and short-tempered, and did not suffer fools gladly. So, inspired by Father Dylan and wee Baby J, I resolved to change.

When I became annoyed with Benni for choosing the longest route possible when I was late for an audition, I would take a breath and remind myself that he was the one doing all the driving.

When I was exasperated with my brother-in-law for constantly disrupting conversations with weak puns and lame dad jokes, I would take a breath and remind myself that he never visited without fixing whatever needed fixing in the house.

When I went ballistic listening to some jackass/asshole/prickhead politician spout untrue and ignorant and racist and woman-hating cow dung, I would take a breath and remind myself…hmm, okay, that was a tough one.

But those resolutions were minor. The new Annie needed to perform an awe-inspiring act of kindness, because even in acts of virtue, I still feel the need to compete. I decided to bring a box of holiday cookies to a bunch of unhoused people who hung out in our local park. To be perfectly honest, I really didn't like having those vagrants there. They were filthy and menacing, and when our home was burglarized, the cops said the thief was probably one of the local homeless guys.

But new Annie wanted to show empathy. I fantasized about delivering my holiday treats to the encampment, making friends, coming home, and finding a package on my doorstep containing the stolen jewelry and iPad and car keys and checkbooks. There would be a note inside the package saying, "Hey, lady. Thanks for the cookies."

And so, moved to tears at the thought of my own goodness, I marched over to the park. When I got there, I discovered that—in the heat of my weepy orgasm of self-love—I had forgotten to pack the cookies. Which was a good thing, because when I passed the filthy, menacing homeless people, I realized that I would never have found to the courage to approach them.

Now some folks would say, "It doesn't matter. It's the thought that counts." And those folks would be dead fucking wrong, because it is *not* the thought that counts, it is the *deed* that counts! But I still believe in Father Dylan's message: "Be kind, be gentle, be tolerant." And from now on, when the holidays roll around, I am going to say to one and all—with all the clarity I can muster, "Merry Christmas!"

A Kosher Muslim

Many years ago, I was seated on a plane next to an MIT student who was flying home to Saudi Arabia for the summer. In those days, you could order special meals, and when we got our food, I was surprised to see that he had ordered a kosher dinner. He explained, "All the Muslim students in Boston shop at kosher butchers, because we can only eat meat that has been blessed by a holy man." Wow! When I rule the world, I will issue a proclamation that we must stop obsessing about our differences and start celebrating our similarities. I am really looking forward to saving mankind.

Misfits

I was writing a book about thrifty living, called *Bargain Junkie*, and had to do a chapter about low-cost entertainment.

> I have a message for the yoga teachers of the world: no class should be longer than one hour.

I saw that Hope Lutheran Church in Hollywood was advertising a free Easter Sunday gospel service. I happen to be a Lutheran enthusiast, because during World War II, the Lutheran church in Denmark was very active in hiding Jews from the occupying Germans. Also, I like gospel music; one of the biggest thrills of my life was being on the same plane as the Blind Boys of Alabama. The Easter Sunday event at the Lutheran church—it was Nazi-haters, a live gospel, and it was free. I'd hit the trifecta!

We were familiar with this church, because we had been to many of their rummage sales, although the vintage clothing I was hoping to find was rarely there. Too many plus sizes, too much polyester. What is it with Gentiles and polyester? Even the poorest Jewish woman wears natural fabrics!

The altar was dominated by a huge wooden cross. That particular cross had been used as a prop in *The Greatest Story Ever Told*, and it just so happened that Benni's friend, the great Swedish actor Max von Sydow, had played Christ in that movie. If I believed that things happen for a reason—which I don't—I would have taken this as another sign that we had chosen the right church.

The people were as welcoming as could be. When someone asked if we were regular members of the congregation, I said, "No, actually, we're Jewish, but we came for the concert."

"Oh, how wonderful, it's so great to have you here!"

And then things started to go downhill.

I turned away for a moment to chitchat with the lady sitting next to me when suddenly she looked up at the altar with a confused expression. There—to my horror—I saw my husband receiving Communion. When he came back to his seat, he explained that he had skipped breakfast and was famished, so he thought that a wafer and a sip of wine seemed like a good idea.

"Have you lost your mind?" I told him. "You have just ingested the body and blood of Christ! You can't treat this sacred ceremony as an opportunity for a *nosh*!"

After the service, there was a reception in the courtyard. Unfortunately, the buffet table featured Rice Krispies marshmallow cookies and peanut butter pies—the polyester of brunch cuisine. Would it kill them to put out a little cheese and fruit?

All during the service, I had been fascinated by a dumpy white woman with two beautiful little Black kids. There was no husband in sight, and she didn't look like she was their natural mother, so I figured she was a single mom who perhaps had adopted from Ethiopia, a popular adoption destination at that time. Jonathan and Alisa were trying to adopt, and I was always looking for more information about the process, so I approached the woman and said, "Excuse me—I'm just wondering—are your lovely children from Ethiopia, by any chance?"

"Certainly not, why would you think that? They're the children of me and my husband."

I had yelled at Benni for treating the sacrament as a *snack*, but could anything have been more insultingly bizarro than what I'd just said here? It was like I was saying, "Excuse me, but you're so terribly unattractive that you couldn't possibly have gotten a gorgeous Black man to have sex with you and create these two magnificent children. Clearly you had to go all the way to Africa to find them." I stuttered and stammered some lame-brained apology, and the woman was a lot more forgiving than I would have been.

Just as I was about to pass out from embarrassment, the minister joined us. He was thrilled to hear about Benni's connection to the prop cross and told us about his upcoming seventh trip to Israel, but was disappointed to hear that we had never been. He clearly liked having Jews in his church, but I don't think we were quite Jewish enough for him. All in all, we might not have been the perfect guests, but it's not easy to fit in when you're different.

That's why I felt concern for my friend Michael's devout Irish Catholic mother on the day she attended Michael's conversion to Judaism. Michael and his partner Cliff are gay…very gay. They look very gay, they talk very gay, they dress very gay. They're also very smart, and very kind, and very funny, but there aren't too many places in the world where they blend in easily. And when Michael decided to join Cliff in being Jewish, he went whole hog, which may not be quite the right metaphor. Michael learned Hebrew, started keeping kosher, sang in the temple choir, and was active on several committees. He and Cliff were probably the two most popular members of the shul.

So, when Michael officially converted, a huge crowd showed up. After the ceremony, there was a buffet lunch, a *real* buffet—thank you very much—with real food: bagels, cream cheese, lox, tuna salad, pasta salad, olives, pickles, cheese, fruit, cookies. As people lined up, Michael's mom was off to one side, chatting with family.

By the time she got to the table, the platters were bare: not a crumb left. No one had explained to the poor thing that—yes—Jews know how to put out a good spread, but they also know how to totally decimate it in seconds like a swarm of hungry locusts. She stood there, in her—you guessed it—Kelly green print polyester dress, with a look of bewilderment that mirrored my puzzlement at the Lutheran peanut-butter-and-marshmallow fiasco. So, I went over and offered to share my mountainous pile of food with her.

I asked how she felt about Michael's conversion, and she said, "I know that my son has found a home in this community, where he is loved and accepted and respected for who he is. Every mother wants that for their child. But I am very sad at the thought that because we now have different faiths, we won't see each other in Heaven."

Michael was standing nearby and overheard this. He came over, put his arm around his mother, and said, "Don't worry, Mom, I'll find you, I promise."

How sweet is that? But I don't believe in Heaven, so I thought: "Why wait?" We all live in our different boxes: the secular box, the Yewish box, the Lutheran, the gay, the Catholic, blah blah blah. But if, once in a while, we dare leave our comfort zone and visit someone else's box, who knows? It might be a little awkward, it might get a little messy, we won't fit right in, but we all just might find each other, right here on Earth. Why wait?

Some Famous Christians

Tennessee Williams was not Jewish. (He was, however, gay, which is almost the same thing.) Jews do not name their children after states. They name them after retail establishments, like Tiffany.

Martha Stewart is not Jewish. No Jewish woman stays home on Saturday night making her own toilet paper.

William Shakespeare was not Jewish, and I can easily prove it: no Jew could write a play called *All's Well That Ends Well.*

6

SPEAKING OUT

Me and my big mouth

Truth to Power

I sincerely believe that the world would be a better place if everyone would just do as I say. I sure couldn't make things worse. When our son was little, we had Miko, a beautiful Swedish au pair, for one year. Miko was seventeen, very timid, very shy, and wasn't always comfortable with my blunt style. We came home one day, and I saw a woman with a huge slobbering dog relieving himself against the front door of our apartment building on Manhattan's Upper West Side.

"Excuse me," I said, "could you please control your animal? People live here!"

"But he's only making wee-wee," the woman said.

"Well, wee-wee is a no-no! So please don't doo-doo that again!"

I looked around for Miko, but she had walked to the end of the block to avoid the fuss.

Another time, we were in Riverside Park when we saw some dumb jerk whacking his little boy on the rear with an umbrella. Miko tried to pull me away—she knew what was coming—but it was too late.

"Excuse me, sir, but you're not allowed to hit your kid. It's against the law!"

"He very bad! He big troublemaker!"

I told the little boy, "If your father beats you, report him to your teacher!"

Dumb jerk lifted his umbrella and came toward me. "You big troublemaker!"

Miko and I ran for our lives.

Many years later, I had a booking for one of my shows in Stockholm, so we looked Miko up. We met in a cafe for some coffee and *kaka*, which is the disgusting Swedish word for "cake." She was still beautiful; she had become a lawyer and was married to a Lutheran minister. But something weird was going on. Everyone in the cafe was staring at us, and various people stopped by our table. They addressed Miko by her real name, Michaela, and shook her hand very respectfully.

She told us, "Everyone in Sweden knows me because of the scandal."

"Scandal? Shy little you? I don't believe it," I said.

She explained that she worked for a huge children's-aid charity. A few years before, she had discovered that the head of the agency was embezzling millions of kroner from the donations. She blew the whistle on him, and her life became a living hell. The man was Sweden's most respected philanthropist. How dare this little nobody question his honesty? The media accused her of being a rejected lover who had made it up to spite him, and some implied that she herself was the one who had stolen the money.

Miko suffered through this nightmare for two years, but she ultimately prevailed, and that great philanthropist went to jail. Today, Michaela is a revered national heroine. Several books have been written about her, and when she goes out in public, people come up to pay their respects.

I found this story amazing, and I told her how proud I was of her. And she said: "I must tell you, Annie, that one thing that helped during my long ordeal was the memory of my time in America. You were the first woman I ever met who wasn't afraid to speak her mind, and that was a great inspiration to me."

Well, how do you like that? I myself have gotten absolutely nowhere by speaking my mind, but look what I did for the country of Sweden. They should give me some kind of reward, like—oh, I don't know—how about the Nobel Prize?

> Anita Hill changed my life. After the way those shithead senators treated her, I have never again trusted white men in suits. (In case you're a white man in a suit, I don't mean you.)

Woman Warrior

One day, my pal Tony asked our poker group to be poll workers on Election Day. I didn't have the time; I was trying to write a new show. I figured I should stay home and work. So, of course, I said my usual "Yeah, why not?" My first task was to go into the booth with an elderly lady who couldn't see very well. As I read the ballot to her, she made choices like, "Simpson? Oh, that's my puppy's name. Let's vote for him." I knew there was a much more qualified candidate running against her pooch, and I was the one pushing the buttons for her. What would you do? I let her have her vote. The puppy won.

A few weeks later, I got one of those scam phone calls. Some guy from an unfamiliar area code wanted me to confirm my Social Security number so they could send me a check. Yeah, right. Like I was that stupid. I told the caller to go fuck himself and called the FBI to report the con. The agent promised to monitor that number.

Later, we went out to dinner with Tony. He said, "Did you get your check?"

"What check?"

"From the Board of Elections. Volunteers are supposed to get paid. They needed your Social Security number, so I told them to call you."

I did not tell Tony that I had reported the Board of Elections to the Feds. In my lifelong battle against injustice, there is sometimes collateral damage.

Angry Comics

I went with a few girlfriends to this little theater in Hollywood where a bunch of comedy writers were doing something called a "spoken word" show. It was mostly personal essays, where people told funny and moving stories about their lives. I had never seen anything like it before, and I was totally mesmerized. Then this guy got up and did a fictional stand-up routine about a whiny *meeskite* (that's Yiddish for an ugly person). The title was "The Little JAP That Could." Really? Are we still mocking Jewish princesses?

The comic was short and balding, with glasses. That's not a put-down; I happen to like that type. Unattractive men make the best lovers, because they try harder. Anyway, I figured I'd just suffer through this jerkoff's act in silence, like I've done a million times before.

Then he read the ugly whiny little JAP's letters home from camp: "I'm finally down to a size one. But these uniforms are lacking in flair, and the counselors are really strict. What-e-verr."

And the big joke was, the ugly little JAP he was talking about was Anne Frank, and the summer camp was Auschwitz. "That train ride really sucked, no air conditioning," the comic went on. "Fortunately, it was an express. Arts and crafts is *so* boring. All we do is take gold out of teeth."

OMG! Had he really just said that? Were people really laughing and clapping? I had to get out of there, but I was stuck way up in a corner, and I couldn't move. My claustrophobia kicked in, big time—cold sweats, palpitations, the works.

And then, finally, one lone person in the audience stood up and shouted, "This is not funny. Get off the stage! You are an abomination!" And it took a moment before I realized that that the lone person was *me*.

The show stopped. Nobody backed me up. People yelled at me to sit down and shut up. My girlfriends, who were polite Midwesterners, pretended they didn't know me, and the comic finished his act to rousing applause.

The next day, I called my old friend Howard in New York.

"Anne Frank? I'm nauseous—nauseous! But don't you worry," he told me. "Everything that goes around comes around, and that little putz has given himself a shitload of bad karma."

I knew Howard meant well, but I don't really buy into that karma crap. A lot of evil is not only unpunished but rewarded. Need I name names? I was so depressed about the whole experience that I medicated myself by spending a week in bed watching reruns of *Frasier*.

Much to my amazement, the producers of the spoken word show invited me to return in a couple of weeks and do a piece explaining my behavior. Now you may wonder why I would even consider going back to that place. That's because you are not a performer. Someone was giving me a chance to take center stage. I would be witty and charming, and everyone would laugh and love me and agree with my point of view, and someone would offer me a job writing and starring in a TV series called *Annie's World*. Martin Short would be a big fan and ask if he can do a guest spot.

Not quite. When word of my scheduled appearance got out, I started getting emails from the comic and his buddies.

"You will be forced offstage in the ugliest way possible, you fascist crone."

"You will die bitter and alone, you humorless hag."

"I'd like to kick you in your withered cunt!"

And then the messages started to get nasty.

"You are the living personification of why Jewish men have contempt for Jewish women."

Oh, great! So now it was all *my* fault? "What should I do?" I wondered. "Should I cancel?" What had I, the world's fraidiest fraidy-cat, gotten myself into? I was getting serious threats of bodily harm from the world's most ruthless terrorist group: angry comics! My friends all advised me this way and that way. Benni said I had to do what felt right to me, but the loudest voice, as always, was the one in my head of my mother, whose lifelong mantra was, "Be careful! Watch out! It could be dangerous!"

Then I remembered that back in the Bronx, Momma had shocked the neighbors in our building by daring to insist that the Rosenbergs did not deserve to be executed. They ganged up on her and accused her of being a dirty communist. They dropped her from the mahjong game, but she refused to back down. And I thought, if my fearful, frightened, phobic mother could find the courage to stand up against a bunch of bullies, maybe I could do the same. So, I decided to reenter the lion's den and have my say.

I couldn't sleep or eat for the weeks leading up to the event—which was great, because I lost a few pounds. We got extra police patrol in case of a disturbance. The theater was packed, the crowd was raucous, and the producers placed a big burly bodyguard to the side of the stage. Ah, the glamour of showbiz!

I spoke. "I believe that comedy is an art, and art is supposed to make you feel good about being alive. But that comic's piece made want to kill myself. And now I need to reveal something: my family is distantly related to the family of Anne Frank." (Which is not true; I made it up. But who gives a fuck?)

Some people applauded; others still accused me of censorship. I don't know if I changed anybody's mind, but the good news is that I did not get beaten up.

And there's more good news. I don't know if Howard was right about that karma crap. I don't know if that comic had to spend every day of the rest of his life prepping for a colonoscopy—although I sincerely hope so—but the night I presented my case was the first time I ever participated in a storytelling event. I discovered then that performing my own words is my true vocation. And so, one of the worst things that ever happened to me turned out to be one of the best things that ever happened to me. Maybe that was *my* karma, and I will be forever grateful to that scuzzy comic and his friends for helping me find it. *Namaste!*

7

PHOBIC-OLOGY

You can live in fear and still have fun

Phobaholic

My favorite sound is not a baby laughing or a gentle summer rain. My favorite sound is that ding on a plane indicating that the seatbelt sign has gone off.

'␣ve had some good results with therapy—mostly when Jonathan was a teenager. It was beneficial to get a little professional guidance during those turbulent years, like how to calmly express my distress when he totaled our car on the way to taking the driver's test.

I had to leave one shrink when I realized that she was insane. It was not so much that I left; it was more like I was thrown out. One of the clauses in our therapeutic contract was that I should always honestly express my feelings about her. One day, I pointed out that although she was a very trendy fashion plate, her taste in art was not so sophisticated. I was referring to a schmaltzy painting in her office of a fluffy little kitten curled up in a wicker basket.

She jumped up from her chair, ripped my check in half, and screamed, "I do not need to sit here and take this abuse. Get out!" The issue we had been working on at the time was my sensitivity to criticism.

But mostly, I've used therapy to try to control my fears, which cover a wide gamut. All I've ever wanted is for everyone I love to *stay in the house*, because it's a dangerous world out there. You see a beach, I see shark attacks. You see a zit, I see melanoma. You say "tomato" and I say "carcinogenic pesticides."

I'm afraid that when I replace the toilet paper, my finger will get caught in that springy thingy. I'm afraid that when I'm at the hairdresser, I will lean too far back into the sink and damage an artery in my neck, which will cause a stroke. Don't laugh, that's a real thing. It's called salon stroke. Look it up!

But my biggest, worst, all-consuming fear is claustrophobia. I cannot be in a crammed elevator. I cannot be in a packed subway car. I cannot be stuck in a crowd. I once marched in a police-brutality protest, but the streets were mobbed, and I suddenly freaked out and had to be rescued by a kindly policeman.

I've tried all kinds of phobia cures. One common technique is positive imagery. You focus on a pleasant place and associate it with the thing that you are afraid of. This is a gigantic load of cow poo. I cannot be in a jam-packed subway train that is stalled in a tunnel under the East River and pretend that I am relaxing on a tropical beach. I know where I am. I am in a jam-packed subway train that is stalled in a tunnel under the East River, and I am going to die.

So, I created the opposite therapy for myself, which I call *negative* imagery. When I am in a scary situation, I think of an even scarier situation, and that gives me some perspective. I am only in a jam-packed subway train that is stalled in a tunnel under the East River. I am not in a cattle car heading toward Auschwitz. I know it seems morbid, but I find it comforting.

Then one day, I just stopped fighting it. Why don't I just accept my flaws? Where is it written that I have to be comfortable in tight spaces? Here's a novel idea: why don't I just avoid the things that terrify me? Crowded subway? I can wait for the next train. Packed elevator? I can walk up a few flights of stairs. Mobbed protest march? I can send a donation.

I decided then that I would never again apologize to anyone for my fears, starting with my own family. A few years later, we were in L.A. and college student Jono announced he was going to Vegas for the weekend with some friends.

"Really? And how, may I ask, are you getting there?"

(Lengthy sigh expressing contempt for the imbecile parent.) "In Dave's car—it's right outside."

I looked at Dave's car, and I saw *death*. It was an open jeep, with no roof and no sides.

"If you take that car through the desert, not only will you be burned to a crisp, but you won't have any protection in a collision," I told Jono. "Why don't you rent a nice four-door sedan?"

"Mo-therrr, you can't cruise girls in a nice four-door sedan."

"You can't cruise girls in a hospital bed!"

"Would you please relax? Why must you always be such a worrier?

"Because I am a worrier! Live with it. Here's some money. Rent a real car!"

The boys were driving back from Vegas, and there was a van in front of them with a heavy glass door strapped to the roof. Suddenly the glass door came loose, flew through the air, and crashed right on top of the rented car. The heavy steel roof protected the kids, and *nobody got hurt*! Ladies and gentlemen, I rest my case.

Glossophobia

This is the only instructional chapter in the book, so you can skip it if you don't need help in this area. But even if you think you don't, you probably do, so do yourself a favor and stay on this page. The number one phobia in America is the fear of public speaking, aka glossophobia. It is just about the only thing in the world that I am *not* afraid of. There are all kinds of cures circulating; the most widespread one is to picture the audience without any clothes on. This is bogus, bullshit, baloney. How can you be up on a podium in front of a large crowd, laboring to remember your words, struggling to get those words out of your mouth and trying to recall how to inhale, while at the same time attempting to visualize something that isn't there? You can't.

But the good news is that even if you have the world's worst case of PSP (public speaking phobia—I just made that up), you can still do a pretty good job. Here are some valuable tricks of the trade that I developed over the years. I usually charge for this kind of instruction, so if these tips bring you some success, I think it's only fair that you send me some money.

1. **Pretend you're someone else.** I was asked to coach a bunch of book authors on reading their work out loud.

They didn't have to memorize the material, and we were just a small, friendly group so I didn't expect any serious problems. Wrong. One woman—an excellent writer—started to read. Her voice was a timid whisper, and her hands shook convulsively. She stopped midway and declared, in tears, that she was too nervous to continue. I asked her if she could think of anyone she admired as being a gifted public speaker. She chose Barack Obama. I asked her to give her piece another try, only this time she should not do it as her herself, but she should try to imitate Obama. She did, and her voice was strong, her bearing relaxed. It was one of the more successful readings of the day. Your nervous system is not as smart as it thinks; it is easily fooled. Just fake it till you make it.

2. **Drill, drill, drill.** Memorize the text, then practice saying it several times day, sometimes at a natural tempo, and sometimes as rapidly as possible. Practice it lying in bed, practice it walking around the block, practice it sitting on the can. Repeat, repeat, repeat. Boring, boring, boring, but all that drudgery will pay off in the end, because you will feel 200 percent secure that you know your text. As with learning a foreign language, mastering a musical instrument, or shooting a basketball, repetition leads to success. I will repeat that because it is so brilliant: repetition leads to success.

3. **Get yourself ready.** Don't eat any heavy food or drink any alcohol before the event. I once had some nachos and a beer before performing in a storytelling contest. I did not win. Maybe because the microphone picked up

the farts. Water is always good, plus you should lubricate your pipes with cough drops or honey-lemon tea. Right before you go on, find a place where you can take a bunch of deep breaths, jump around, wave your arms, and shake your hands to calm your nerves and get those juices flowing. Now march around to your favorite upbeat song (I like Gloria Gaynor's "I Will Survive") to put you in touch with your ruler-of-the-world self.

4. **Yell from the belly.** When you're feeling nervous and shy, your breathing gets shallow, and your vocal energy takes a nose-dive. So, while you're giving your talk, breathe deep and speak as loud as a preacher—even if you're miked. A strong voice will convince your audience—and your gullible nervous system—that you are a fearless speaker.

You can send me a check in care of my publisher.

8

THE FINER THINGS

Culture vulture

Dinner and a Show

There is a place that combines inspirational language, stirring music, and a transcendent connection to the people around you. It is a place where you get flashes of ecstasy, moments of heavenly bliss. You might call that place church. I call it a Broadway musical. Theater is one of life's most magical pleasures. Why? Because the actors are *alive*! You're sharing a thrilling experience with people who are *alive*! And the music is not canned, it is *live*! I'm not just talking about plays. I'm talking about concerts, operas, dance recitals, stand-up clubs, improv groups, jazz festivals, and spoken-word shows. And, yeah, circuses and magic acts and strip clubs. Well, maybe not strip clubs.

What I just said about enriching your life with the performing arts is so inspiring, I wish I had the guts to do it. I'm just talking the talk; I am a total fraud. The sad truth is that I *used* to be a really cultured person. When we lived in New York, we went to all those plays and ballets and lectures. Then we moved to L.A. The traffic.

The parking. The challenge of finding somewhere to eat after a show. It is just so much easier to stay home, order takeout, and binge-watch *The Mindy Project*. So do as I say, not as I do.

Two things I could live without:

1. Frank Sinatra singing "My Way."
2. Judy Collins singing "Send in the Clowns."

Books: Why?

I studied script interpretation with the great Stella Adler of the Group Theater. When we read *The Glass Menagerie*, she said that most actors play Tom, the poet, as a weakling.

"Wrong," she said. "The writer is always a man of strength, because he's the one with real insight into human nature."

Good old Stella was right on the money.

If you want to understand women, read *Pride and Prejudice*. If you want to understand children, read *All the Light We Cannot See*. If you want to understand men, read *The Great Gatsby*. Forget facts and figures; when I am named ruler of the earth, I will decree that all politicians be required to read the world's one hundred greatest books. Maybe then they will finally understand what buttholes they are and change their evil ways.

I don't understand most of the cartoons in *The New Yorker*. Is it me, or is it them?

Movies: Chick Flicks and Dick Flicks

Most films are made by men, are about men, and get reviewed by men. This is not good news for me, because I am a grown woman who cringes at fight scenes, falls asleep during action sequences, and walks out during macho revenge tales. I'm all for keeping in touch with your inner child, as long as that child is not a male adolescent.

Here are the words that will keep me away from any movie: "grim," "dystopian," "harrowing," "nonstop action," "brutality," "special effects," "war," "prison."

Here are the words that will make me want to see a movie: "witty," "hilarious," "literate," "enchanting," "gritty," "suspenseful," "moving," "powerful," "poignant," "entertaining," "satisfying," "intelligent."

Here are some of my personal faves, besides the obvious ones like *E. T.*, *The Godfather* trilogy, and *Rocky*.

- *Enchanted April*
- *The Secret Life of Walter Mitty* (2013)
- *Babette's Feast* (full disclosure: Benni's partner produced it)
- *The Descendants*
- *The Band Wagon*
- *Little Miss Sunshine*
- *Silver Linings Playbook*

These films all pass my three-H test: Heart, Humor, and a Happy ending. (*Babette's Feast* lacks humor but is profoundly moving, so it made the cut.)

Watch them, and for each one that you love, please send me one dollar. I'm doing a crowdfunding campaign for a Mediterranean cruise.

I overheard an elderly German woman complaining that they shouldn't make movies about the Holocaust because it puts her country in a bad light.

TV Rules!

Occasionally, I run into someone who says, with great pride, "Oh, we never watch television." I do not tell these people that they are ignorant, pretentious snob shits, because I am a lady. We are living in the Golden Age of television: the writing, the acting, and the understanding of humanoid behavior are what we used to get from the movies, when movies were for grown-ups. And it is not just American TV that I'm addicted to; it's also Israeli, Danish, Korean, Irish, and many more.

> How is it possible that Carol Burnett never hosted *Saturday Night Live*?

I am so thankful I didn't live in those days gone by when most activities ended when the sun went down. Some of my happiest hours have been spent well after midnight as I laugh at *The Big Bang Theory*, cry at *This Is Us*, bite my nails at *The Sopranos*, and am spellbound by *NYPD Blue*. It sure beats lighting a candle and catching up on my weaving.

> I used to love sex—until I got Roku. Which would I rather have: an orgasm or *House Hunters International*? I think you know the answer.

The News: A How-To Manual of Bad Behavior

People believe whatever you tell them about themselves, so when my grandson, Max, was a baby, I repeatedly assured him that he was smart, beautiful, gentle, and kind. And that, of course, is what he has turned out to be. Likewise, if you repeatedly tell a kid that he's a stupid, worthless piece of shit, chances are you will not get a Rhodes Scholar; you probably won't even get a decent, average, everyday person. What you will probably get is a stupid, worthless piece of shit.

Which leads us to the news: I do not like the news, because it keeps telling us how evil we are and, just like kids, we ingest the message and do what's expected of us. If they broadcast a rise in anti-Semitic violence, I guarantee you the result will be a surge of anti-Semitic violence.

On the other hand, if they ran a story saying, "Statistics prove that the USA. is the most racially tolerant nation in the world," I bet a lot of bigots would throw out their white hoods and jump on the tolerance bandwagon.

> When I am in charge of everything, I will demand that every citizen be exposed to opposing points of view. If you're a Laura Ingraham fan, you must give equal time to Joy Behar.

So, I would like to create a twenty-four-hour news station that reports only good news—like the Pakistani-born restaurant owner who gives a free meal to anyone who needs it, or the rural schoolteacher who takes a second job to buy school supplies for her students. When I am empress of the earth, I will expose every living human to daily news accounts of empathy and generosity. My TV programming will create world peace. You're welcome.

My questions for any presidential candidate:

Do you have a degree in law, public affairs, history, or political science?

What's your favorite book? Movie? TV show?

What is your spouse's profession?

When is the last time you were moved to tears?

How many friends do you have who are not rich, white Christians?

9

TALES OF MANY CITIES

New York, Los Angeles, Copenhagen, and the rest of the world

I asked Max what he loves most about visiting New York.

"The subway!"

"That's odd. What do you like about it?"

"Waiting for the train."

Seriously? Waiting for a train is not my idea of a good time, but I think I get it: Max is enjoying the anticipation of the sudden roar of the engine, the bright lights cutting through the dark station, and the huge energy of that giant machine suddenly entering our space. This child has perfected the art of living in the moment.

Bites of the Big Apple

I live in one of those newly hip L.A. neighborhoods. We've got a silent movie theater, vegan cafes, and a dance studio called Yoga Booty Ballet. It's kind of cool, kind of urban, but it's still a New York wannabe and a poor substitute for the real thing. We moved here many years ago, but I still suffer from Manhattan Island withdrawal and get back whenever I can.

For one thing, I miss seeing less-than-perfect people on the street. You are not allowed to be old or dowdy or fat in Los Angeles, and you must dress like a teenager even if you're decades past being one. The mature professional woman in a well-tailored pantsuit and a vintage brooch is a cringey look here, despite *The Good Wife*, but it's okay for a granny to wear ripped jeans.

I miss the levelheaded rationalism of New Yorkers. Angelenos buy into every fad that mumbo-jumbo pseudo science can offer—from placenta pills to high colonics. I bought a crystal necklace at a yard sale, and the seller advised me to rinse it in salt water as soon as I got home.

"Why should I do that? Does salt water brighten the sparkle?" I asked.

"No, it will remove my aura."

That sounded like a good idea to me. I would definitely not want to be anywhere near her aura.

> I met a professional psychic at a Hollywood party who told me that her husband had died unexpectedly. She was a psychic; shouldn't she have expected it?

I miss smart-ass New York sarcasm. I was once shopping for a specific recipe and stupidly asked the greengrocer for two shallots.

"*Two* shallots?" he says. "You expecting company, maybe?"

I miss all the different ways that New Yorkers connect with each other. Friends run into each other on the street and stop to chat. Neighbors meet in the elevator and stop to chat. One woman I know noticed a cute guy on the subway who was reading a book she liked. They started chatting, and a year later they got married. I doubt that any love matches have originated between drivers on the 405 freeway.

I was once at the bread counter at Zabar's—Manhattan's legendary specialty-food emporium—and overheard an older Jewish woman ask the Puerto Rican counter man, "Pedro, did you get your daughter that book I told you about?"

Compare that to the L.A. Whole Foods, where I saw a white, Armani-clad dude say to the Black counter guy who was handing dude his quinoa salad, "Thank you, mah bruthah."

Bruthah's forced smile looked like it made his face hurt.

And speaking of food, here's a very partial list of New York basics almost impossible to find in L.A.: cold sesame noodles, toasted corn muffins, chocolate egg creams, crusty pumpernickel bread, onion rolls, and a Greek coffeeshop grilled cheese sandwich. And let us not forget Gray's Papaya hot dogs on 72nd Street. They tried opening a NY-style Papaya King in Hollywood, but they neglected to grill the buns. A hot dog nestled in a cold, slightly damp bun is an affront to mankind. I miss the neighborhood delis where you can grab a tuna sandwich, a cold beer, and a dozen roses in less time than it takes to pay for a bag of chips in oh-so-slow-and-laid-back L.A.

I miss the New York parks. In Los Angeles, most middle-class and up folks stay in their own backyards, so the parks are largely inhabited by blue-collar families. New York parks, on the other hand, are shared by the rich and poor alike, and they are full of human drama—like the kite-flying contest in Central Park where we watched a contestant get disqualified because he had attached razors to his kite string to cut off the strings of other kites. Fun!

And then there are the countless unexpected captivating moments every New Yorker has experienced. I once stepped into the Times Square subway station and was greeted by the sublime sounds of a Mozart string quartet played by a rainbow coalition of young Juilliard students—much more magical than the guy who juggles a chain saw on L.A.'s Venice Beach.

Speaking of buskers, a long time ago, I was strolling through a street fair on Manhattan's Amsterdam Avenue when I came to a platform where a Latin band was blasting away with horns, drums, keyboard, and congas. The rhythms were irresistible, and everyone on the street was dancing. I thought, "These guys are pretty impressive to be playing at a street fair."

Then I got a little closer and recognized the band leader: Tito Puente. For free. On the sidewalks of New York.

I will admit that there are a few things I do appreciate about L.A.: the pleasant climate, the hummingbirds outside my window, the year-round yard sales. And there's also my wide circle of loving friends (mostly ex-Manhattanites) and my enjoyable work—in other words, my life. But just like you don't have to believe in God to be Jewish, you don't have to still live on 84th and West End to be a New Yorker.

When I am in charge of everything, here's how I will easily improve traffic and housing conditions in New York.

Any driver who blocks an intersection gets a two-hundred-dollar ticket, and if they do it again, their license will be suspended for a year and they will be exiled to the burbs.

Anyone who pays over $3 million for an apartment should have to kick in another million to the city for the purpose of building affordable housing. (Two million if the buyer is not a U.S. citizen.)

Eviction Notice

In 2016, Benni and I were evicted from the Los Angeles home we had loved for many years. Always the cheerful optimist, my response was suicidal. You see, when I was a child, I learned the importance of house pride, because I grew up with the opposite: house shame.

My childhood home was a three-room railroad flat in the Bronx. I hated the apartment, and I hated the Bronx. I was already a little snob-in-training, and I hated that all the blue-collar Jews on Mosholu Parkway looked alike, talked alike—they even ate alike! Italian on Friday, deli on Saturday, Chinese on Sunday. Plus, Mosholu was a long, tortuous, subway ride from everything I was interested in: museums, Greenwich Village, and Broadway shows.

Our apartment was cramped and crowded and depressing. The tiny hallway was taken up by a sewing machine where my father did alterations, which just added to the general clutter. My one refuge was my dollhouse. I placed an antique chandelier over the dining room table, a Persian rug on the floor, and red velvet curtains on the windows. That's where I first discovered that make-believe is a much happier place than the real world.

When I was around nine years old, an upright piano was delivered by way of the fire escape. On our block, no matter how humble the dwelling, there was always room for a piano. A Jewish mother's success was measured in how well her child played Beethoven's *Für Elise*. Luckily for me, I played it very well, and that was my ticket out of the Bronx. *Danke*, Ludwig.

I got into the High School of Music & Art, which was in… *Manhattan*! And it got me invited to parties with kids who did not have sewing machines in their hallways. Kids who had parents who spoke English as their first language. Kids who lived in huge apartments on West End Avenue with grand pianos in the living rooms.

When I became a married lady, Benni and I moved into our own apartment on West End Avenue. The first thing I did was hang an antique chandelier over the dining table and place a Persian rug on the floor, red velvet curtains on the windows, and a baby grand in the living room. I was living the dream.

And then there were the neighbors. Jono would play with the rich kid in 5C, Benni would practice his German with the concert pianist in 12A, and the gay guys in 3B would host quiche brunches once a month. If we strolled around the corner for dinner and a movie, we would always bump into someone we knew. It was like living in small-town America—without the racists.

In 1990, we moved to Los Angeles. There were no people in the streets, the restaurants closed at nine-thirty, and the bagels…had blueberries.

But we did have a lovely home. There was no room for a grand piano, but I was fine with a small spinet in the office/guest room. Yes, I had an office, Benni had an office, and we had a dining room and a breakfast room and a laundry room and a front yard and a back yard. *Nice*! And then one day the walls came tumbling down: the building got sold, and the new owner had plans for the property that did not include us. We were given twelve months to relocate.

Now what? We wanted to stay in the same neighborhood, but rents had skyrocketed since we first moved in. Our only choice was "downsizing." But hold on a second! I am all about "upsizing"! Downsizing would mean the death of my lifestyle.

No more garden parties, no more out-of-town guests, no walk-in closets, and only one bathroom. We would end up in a cramped, cluttered, depressing space. We would end up—God help me—in *the Bronx!*

Look, I know that this is a first-world problem. I know that most people on the planet don't own a book or a toilet, and that I should be grateful for whatever I have. But I learned long ago that if I don't love where I live, I cannot be happy. And—call me shallow—I happen to like happiness.

An acquaintance reproached me for being so materialistic. "Why are you making such a tragedy out of this? I could live in a trailer park just as long as Robert was with me." The bitch resided in a five-thousand-square-foot house in Bel-Air with a screening room and a manmade waterfall. Don't you just love it when wealthy people tell unwealthy people that money isn't everything?

I couldn't sleep. I couldn't digest my food. I got daily attacks of nausea, dizziness, and racing heartbeats, which—with the help of Dr. Google—I promptly diagnosed as a series of strokes. My physician said I was just suffering from anxiety, and he suggested I try meditating. He was kidding, right? Let me tell you something about meditation: meditation only works if you're in a good mood!

So, I did what any sensible person would do: I went to a hypnotist. I listened to a tape of our session every day.

"I am resourceful. I am brave. I can solve this problem."

"I am resourceful. I am brave. I can solve this problem."

Clearly, it was a load of gobbledygook, but my ignorant unconscious mind was dumb enough to believe it, so I began to sleep again. I began to breathe again. And I began preparing for the move, which was a daunting task.

For starters, we had to dissolve two home businesses, which meant figuring out how the hell to unload ten thousand rare books and two garages jam-packed with hundreds of pieces of vintage fashion. Plus, there were all our personal treasures: tribal masks, Chinese Deco rugs, vintage California pottery (all picked up on the cheap at garage sales and thrift stores). I held yard sales, I took ads on Craigslist, I sold online. It turned out that all the stuff we had amassed over the years was a lot more valuable than we knew. It was pretty satisfying to get $1,200 for a piece of Japanese calligraphy that had cost us forty bucks. The dreaded move was beginning to have the teensiest weensiest element of...*pleasure*!

We were forced to do a thorough reorganization of our offices, and even this had an element of fun, because it was very liberating to get rid of mountains of papers that were—perhaps—not worth saving. Like a 1996 receipt from Goodwill for a $3.75 wastebasket.

Now all we had to do was find a new home. We had a wide choice—of one. The only option was a rent-controlled community a few blocks away. We had to submit an itemized personal, professional, and financial history beginning at birth, and I am someone who needs help filling out a W-4 form. We had to find proof of this and proof of that. Copies of this and copies of that.

"I am resourceful. I am brave. I can solve this problem."

"I am resourceful. I am brave. I can solve this problem."

Wrong, I couldn't. But Benni could, which reminded me of one of the things I like about being married. When you're feeling helpless in the face of a calamity, it's nice to have some backup.

After many months of bureaucratic hell, we finally got approved for a two-level townhouse—not quite as large as the one we were vacating, but a lot bigger than that railroad flat in the Bronx. Big enough to still have houseguests and garden parties (patio parties would be more accurate). And—what a shocker!—for the first time since we left New York, we had neighborly neighbors. When Benni had hip surgery, our bell rang every day with offers of chicken curry from the Indian family, home-baked challah from the Orthodox Jews, and mac and cheese from the Midwesterners. My favorite thing in the world is free food. Would it be very wrong if I pretended to have cancer?

The house is in one of L.A.'s few walkable neighborhoods, so, once again, we can stroll around the corner for dinner and a movie, and chances are that we will bump into someone we know. Once again, it's like living in small-town America—without the assault weapons.

There are folks who believe that when something bad happens, something good always follows. I am not one of those folks. I think that even when something *good* happens, there is a good chance it will end badly. But in this case, those asinine chirpy optimists were right. The eviction that I thought was a life-destroying disaster turned out to be an astonishing stroke of good luck.

9/11: I'm Glad I Was There

Every year, on September 11, I put on my "I ♥ NY" T-shirt and wear it with pride all day. We were living in L.A. at that time but had flown into the Big Apple for a booking of one of my solo shows. Most people associate that catastrophe with hatred, bloodshed, and terrorism. Not me. I associate it with generosity, compassion, and heroism.

When the towers fell, we ran down to donate blood. The lines were blocks long, and everyone waited patiently to do their part. This in itself was a heroic act, because New Yorkers are not known for waiting patiently. There would be no recipients for that blood, but we didn't know the full details of the tragedy yet. Folks just wanted to show their support in any way they could.

Some therapist friends offered free counseling for grief-stricken firemen who had lost their coworkers. A few people I knew went down to Ground Zero every day to help prepare food for the first responders. Our buddy Mike Spera was an executive at Kaufman Astoria Film Studios in Queens. He called the mayor's office and said, "I've got all kinds of equipment. Whaddaya need?" He then arranged for the delivery of giant HMI lights and cranes to Ground Zero. The lighting that was normally used to make movies was now allowing the search efforts to continue through the night. Showbiz met community service in a really meaningful way.

Our friend Phil called to say, "We got chicken. Ya comin' over?" Dinner that night, and most nights for the weeks that followed, was for a crowd. We all needed to stay connected. On the sidewalks, you would pass people greeting each other, embracing, and then asking, "Is everything okay?" which was code for, "Did you lose anyone?" In supermarkets, at bus stops, on bank lines, total strangers would strike up conversations. We spoke to one young couple from Kentucky who had jumped into their pickup and come to New York for the first time in their lives, just to see if they could be of any help. I asked if they were going to do any sightseeing as long as they were here. Oh, definitely—they already had their tickets for a Smackdown Wrestling Event at Madison Square Garden. Those were sweet kids; I will not judge.

Every restaurant, bar, and coffeeshop was full to capacity. If a first responder entered, we all stood up and applauded. After that week, I had a much higher regard for men in uniform. You have to respect people whose job description includes the possibility of dying.

While this global drama was unfolding, there was my own little crisis in my own little life. I was scheduled to do a show on September 16 at Queens College. We considered canceling, but our producer decided to go ahead since we already had decent presales. However, people were still healing and were unlikely to be in a let's-go-see-an-unknown-actress-in-a-solo-performance-piece mood, so we prepared ourselves for lots of no-shows and a half-empty theater.

Well, not only did we sell out, but there was a long list of people hoping for last minute cancellations. Let's be clear here. They were not there to see *me*. They were there to see *anybody*! They wanted to laugh, they wanted to forget, they wanted to escape the endless TV coverage of the attack. And like all egocentric performers, I like to think that I provided a little comfort to some wounded souls.

Denmark, My Country-in-Law: The Bad, the Good, and the Beautiful

The Bad

I've been married to a Dane for many years. I've lived and worked in Copenhagen, I've traveled around the country, and I speak the difficult language—which the Danes themselves refer to as a "disease of the throat." (Well, I *think* I speak the language. Friends and family might not agree.)

We hear a lot of talk these days about Danish *hygge*: the concept of creating a snug, cozy atmosphere featuring numerous glowing candles and the pleasant company of a few close friends. (BTW, that word, "*hygge*," cannot be pronounced if your tongue was born outside of Scandinavia. The closest pronunciation would be "*huey/guh*") Some suspect that their *hygge* lifestyle is the reason that Danes are among the happiest people in the world.

Hygge takes place in a placid, serene atmosphere. You're not aiming for frenzied high spirits; you just want a feeling of quiet contentment. And when it comes to quiet, Danes are world champs. At the Royal Theatre, at seaside cafes, at country inns, people converse in the hushed whispers of a memorial service.

Anyway, I am here to tell you that this whole happy-*hygge*-let's-all-be-Danes craze is based on a smelly pile of BS. For starters, that "happiness" thing is a false positive. In Denmark, expressing, sharing, or discussing negative feelings of any kind is the eighth deadly sin, so few Danes would ever admit to being *un*happy.

Also, Scandinavians live according to a principle called the Jante Law—which is pronounced "Yenta Law" but is the total opposite of any self-respecting yenta's belief system. This law forbids being outspoken, ambitious, or competitive, or expressing any pride in your accomplishments. You are never supposed to be better than your neighbor. The typical response to anyone with big dreams is, "Who do you think you are?"

This is a culture of low expectations, so any piddling little pleasure—like the sun coming out for a few minutes—is cause for celebration. Preferably accompanied by booze. Oh, did I mention that Danes drink a lot? A lotta lot. Which is not something that happy people do. You'd drink too if you lived in a place where the climate ranges from really shitty to not quite as shitty, and the most popular side dish is boiled potatoes.

Since Danes don't expect much, they are willing to put up with all kinds of inconveniences. Homes are built without closets, and bathrooms are built without storage space. Maybe that's the reason Danish women don't wear much makeup: there's no place to put it. On the other hand, they always find room for a bidet. I don't get it. If space is so limited, how about an extra washcloth instead of a piece of furniture?

Danes will go to great lengths to avoid drama. Most weddings—for those who bother to get married—don't have processionals. Brushing away tears as the bride walks down the aisle to the strains of beautiful music would be much too sentimental. There are even families who do not have funerals for their loved ones: "Death comes to everyone, let's not get all maudlin about it."

Danes worship at the altar of the plain, the simple, and the "natural." Aging is "natural."

Older women live out their golden years sporting mannish gray haircuts and shapeless gray raincoats. Maybe some Americans overdo the "forever young" thing, but sometimes a little pizazz is a welcome sign of life. Bring on that statement necklace!

Sex is "natural." The Danes are very free and easy about fornication, nudity, all that stuff. Women are topless at the beach, and little kids run around naked in the park. I first went to Denmark during the sexual revolution. Benni was producing a film about the Danish porno industry, so we went to this little club in a seedy part of town to watch a live sex show. We sat there with a busload of Japanese businessmen while this young couple performed twenty minutes of gymnastic copulation. They did it standing, they did it sitting, they rolled on the floor, they hung upside down. I had never felt so hopelessly untalented.

After the show, we went backstage to interview them, but they couldn't stay and talk. They had to be at work early in the morning. Because they were kindergarten teachers. They were only doing the sex clubs to earn money for a washer and dryer.

Sexual relationships among the Danes are very fluid. Couples break up and hook up with others and break up again with such frequency that if I run into someone I haven't seen in a while, I always hesitate to send regards home because I'm never sure who occupies home at that moment. One woman I know married her ex-husband's brother. Another guy was sleeping with his best friend's wife. He felt guilty about being dishonest, so he dutifully informed the friend about what was going on. The friend immediately left his wife—not because she was cheating on him, but because she hadn't been honest enough to tell him. The two men remained best friends. I do not understand any part of that story.

But the Danes are not always so loosey-goosey. They have a psychotic respect for authority, and *always* obey the rules. If the light is red, a Dane will not cross the street. Denmark is a flat country, and you can see all the way to Germany that there are no cars coming. But they will stand in the freezing rain and wait for permission to go.

There is no concept of *service* in Denmark. Waiters take forever to bring your food, and then they disappear for the next hour, so if they forgot to bring ketchup for the fries, you will have to eat those fries without ketchup, which, as we all know, is inhuman. The bakery clerk slowly wraps each loaf of bread, totally oblivious to the long line of patiently waiting customers. When our Danish family and friends come to L.A. for a visit, they go into culture shock.

"We walked into a store, and they said, 'Hi, how are you today?' And then they helped me find what I needed," they'll relate in awe. "Can you believe it?"

In a society where you follow the rules, don't make waves, and avoid emotional extremes, therapy is not a big seller. Danes are very disapproving of people who choose to revisit the ordeals of their childhoods. This is a culture that champions the unexamined life, so people keep making the same self-destructive choices over and over and over.

Okay, enough with the kvetching. I have now expressed more complaints than most Danes would voice in a lifetime. Let's move on to the cheerier stuff.

The Good

Danish food culture has developed beyond boiled potatoes in recent years. My brother-in-law makes a mean Thai coconut soup. And those sixty-five-year-old frumps who look eighty are strong, capable women who cheerfully dig in their gardens and bake their bread and bike to their volunteer work at the local community center.

From an early age, Danes are taught decency, honesty, and empathy. That humanistic attitude is reflected in their social system. Maybe the size of your bathroom is not so important when you have free education, free healthcare, free daycare, free old-age care, fifty-two weeks' shared maternity leave, and six weeks' paid vacation every year—which many spend in not-too-shabby places like Greece, Spain, and the Maldives.

There are no homeless encampments, because there are no homeless. There are no shootings, because there are no guns. There are no school massacres, because disturbed children are diagnosed early on and given proper treatment. Imagine that!

Danes may not be as happy as we've been told, but they sure as hell seem content with their lot—and for good reason.

The Beautiful

One night, we were visiting some friends of Benni's parents in a tranquil (by which I mean deadly dull) suburb of Copenhagen. The conversation was boring beyond belief, and I was desperate to find something to talk about besides the price of herring—so I complimented the couple on their excellent English and asked if they'd studied it in school. There was an awkward silence.

"Eh, no, actually, we learned it during the war."

"Really? But Denmark was occupied by the Nazis. Seems like a strange time to learn English."

Again, they hesitated. I sensed the subject was making them uncomfortable, so of course, I pursued it.

"How come you learned English during the war?"

"Uh, we had someone living here who spoke English."

"I don't understand."

"Well, it's not something we like to make a fuss about. Our guest was a British RAF pilot who had been shot down, and we hid him in our basement for two years. Would you like some more liver?"

Holy crapoli! And I'd thought they were just a boring old couple. Well, they *were* a boring old couple—who also happened to be incredibly heroic. And they were not the only ones; almost all of Denmark's Jews had been saved by the efforts of private citizens who'd felt it was "the right thing to do."

The fugitives had to be hidden in small fishing boats and sailed across the Øresund to Sweden. The waters were treacherous, and the Sound was filled with German patrol boats. Benni's parents were among the fugitives. They were not sure they would survive the trip, so they contacted some friends who lived in the countryside. The Nielsens, who were pious Christians, agreed to hide little Benni from the Nazis. He was told to tell people that his name was Nielsen, and that he was their nephew from Copenhagen.

Oddly enough, Benni remembers this as a happy and exciting time. He was a city child, and the big, old-fashioned garden was a magical place for him. The two little Nielsen girls showed him how to dig new potatoes out of the ground, and they played hide-and-go-seek for hours at a time. Every day, Benni went to the baker to buy himself a treat.

One day he took the baker aside and whispered, "I'll tell you a big secret. My real name isn't Nielsen. It's Korzen, but nobody's supposed to know!" Instead of reporting them to the local German commandant, the baker went to the Nielsens and warned them that their "nephew" was talking too much. On a dark, moonless night, some young members of the Underground picked Benni up, and they sailed across the Øresund to his parents, who had arrived safely in Sweden.

Twenty-two years later, Benni was working as a production assistant/translator on a CBS documentary about the rescue of the Danish Jews. They were interviewing a bookbinder in Elsinore who had been a member of the Underground, and he was getting tired of all the questions. He told Benni in Danish to get the fucking Americans out of there already. Then a neighbor stopped by, and when he heard Benni's name, he said to the bookbinder, "Korzen? Didn't we sail a little boy named Korzen over to Sweden? And didn't his father give us all inscribed silver cigarette cases?"

Once the bookbinder realized who Benni was, his grumpiness turned into jovial hospitality. He ordered beer and aquavit for all, and the Danes and the fucking Americans spent the rest of the afternoon celebrating a remarkable reunion.

People Are More Fun Than Churches

I've been to lots of faraway places, and after years of respectfully visiting every museum, castle, and church in the guidebooks, I suddenly began to feel that everything around me was—how can I put it?—*dead*. So, I raced out of the Gothic cathedral and into the supermarket, and I've never looked back.

For me, the true joy of travel can be found in wandering through food courts, pharmacies, and hardware stores. My house is full of foreign loot, like a display of superrealistic plastic sushi I picked up in Tokyo, my Florentine cheese grater, and my midcentury modern Danish toilet brush—the first ever designed to fit into a molded holder. Yes, even poop-stain cleaners can become collectibles.

I've gotten real insights into culture—theirs and ours—just by soaking up everyday commerce. Like the time in Stockholm when the raggedy old man in front of me on the checkout line bought twenty cans of beer and a potato, because the antidrinking laws in Sweden required that you bought food whenever you got booze.

We should try this! How about a law that says every time you buy a ticket for an action movie, you also have to buy a novel written by a woman?

ANNIE KORZEN

Another time, in Nice, I was exploring the local farmer's market, but I wasn't looking at the veggies. I was more fascinated by the French women of all ages and all sizes who did their shopping in the same outfit: strappy stilettos; a short, sexy dress; and a scowl. I could barely walk on those bumpy cobblestone streets without twisting an ankle, but those sullen hoochie mamas click-clacked along without dropping a baguette.

My happiest offbeat tourist moment took place in an upscale suburb of Copenhagen, when Benni's sister asked if I'd like to visit the garbage dump. Yes, you heard me, the garbage dump. But this was no nasty, smelly landfill. It was a clean, well-organized trash depot on a woodsy road. And the kicker was, they had this large wooden A-frame where people put perfectly good things that they were simply tired of, and anyone could just take what they wanted. A frugalista's wet dream! I scored eight Marimekko placemats and a huge orange ceramic teapot. When I am president, every community will erect one of these structures.

Clearly, my brand of off-the-beaten-path tourism is great for people on a budget. It doesn't cost a dime to gawk at the fish heads for sale in Chinatown, or to witness the entire staff bow in formal welcome when a Tokyo department store opens in the morning. Plus, you'll have priceless cultural experiences that could never happen in a museum.

When I was growing up in the Bronx, the motto was "Stick to your own kind." I'm so glad I ignored that suggestion. My life has been made so much richer by the other kind.

I've got nothing against fine art, but there's something to be said for visiting the town dump.

Conquering the Tuscan Lavatory

Benni and I once spent ten days in Tuscany, and it was everything I'd always dreamed of: ancient medieval hill towns, sheep grazing on rolling hills, leisurely meals ending with herb-scented local cheese. Heaven on Earth. But even in heaven, nothing's perfect. Like using the restroom. I learned to allow twenty minutes for what would normally be a three-minute transaction.

Minutes one to five: Finding the light. Europeans are not wasteful of power. You only get light when you need it. I had to feel around in the dark for the switch. I slid my hand along one wall, then another. I waved it in the air in case there was a chain. I looked on the outside, near the door. My Lambrusco-filled bladder was not happy at the delay. Okay, got it.

Minute five: Doing my business.

Minutes six to ten: Flushing. They like to play with you, these Europeans, and the name of the game is "Find the Handle, you Stupida Americana Turista." They make sure that it's nowhere you might logically expect it to be. It's not on top of the commode. It's not on the wall behind the commode. It's not alongside the commode. More likely it's placed on the opposite wall, where you'd never in a million years think of looking.

Minutes ten to fifteen: Unlocking the door to leave the toilet stall. The locks were viciously complicated, and needed two or three moves to come loose. Plus, unlike here at home, the door went from floor to ceiling. The light, as always, was on a timer, so if I didn't get the door open very soon, I would be trapped in a small space, plunged into terrifying darkness. And I'd forgotten the word for "help" in Italian. I fiddled desperately with the lock as I tried to keep breathing.

"I am resourceful. I am brave. I can solve this problem."

"I am resourceful. I am brave. I can solve this problem."

Minutes fifteen to twenty: Using the sink. Okay, I was finally free and needed to wash my hands. There was a faucet but no hot or cold handles. Ha, they didn't get me this time, because I had seen it in the States. All I had to do was place my hands under the faucet, and the sensor would cause water to flow down. I did it. Nothing happened. I moved my hands back and forth. Nothing. Nothing happened, because there was no sensor. Then I jumped out of my skin at the sound of a booming male voice close behind me.

"*Signora*! Down there! Down on the floor!" I looked in the mirror and saw this giant, bearded, Pavarotti type breathing down my neck. I had forgotten the nastiest trick of all: in Italy, the ladies' room is often the ladies' and men's room. I looked down at the floor, and there was a pedal. I stepped on it, and the water gurgled out as I nervously thanked him with three of my five Italian words. "Ha-ha-ha. *Grazie, signore, molte grazie*."

By the time I got back to my table, I was drenched in sweat, everyone was on dessert, and I had a plate of cold ravioli waiting for me. Maybe next time I travel, I'll wear those astronaut diapers.

The French Waiter

I am proud to be an American, but there is a lot of stuff in our culture that I'm kinda snobby about. A Big Mac is my idea of toxic waste, as are Oreos, cupcakes, and jellybeans. I'm nauseated by reality TV, I cringe at Hallmark cards, and I have never, ever, watched a Super Bowl game (except, of course, for the half-time show).

But when I travel, those foreigners don't recognize me as the supersophisticated, classy, urbane creature I think I am. They see me as just another dumb American. I was at a wedding reception in Denmark, and the mother-of-the-bride stood up and tapped her glass.

"I have an announcement. Please forgive me, I know it's raining heavily today, but since we have little children and an American here today, I must ask you all to please smoke outside!"

And, this being Europe, the whole room emptied out.

I try to fit in when I travel abroad. I tolerate the scratchy toilet paper, and I wash my hair by kneeling in the tub and spraying the whole room with an unwieldy shower cord. I force a smile when listening to that puke-making Europop. Every once in a while, though, the real American me is revealed, and it does not receive a warm welcome.

Try asking for decaf in Sicily and you will see what I mean. Or a doggy bag anywhere outside the States. I nearly started an international incident in Belgrade, Serbia, by putting on my safety belt. The cab driver snarled at me, "You tink maybe I not good driver? You tink maybe Americans drive more better den me?"

One night, we were at the Cannes film festival... I'm so impressed with that phrase that I'm going to repeat it. One night, we were at the Cannes film festival, and I was all excited because we were going to a legendary ten-star ooh-la-la-type restaurant. For a poor girl from Mosholu Parkway in the Bronx, I had become a truly glamorous citizen of the world!

The first thing I saw, three feet away from me, sitting at the bar, was a Very Famous Movie Star. I won't mention his name, because you're probably too young to remember James Mason, but I worship this guy! I thought, "Maybe after dinner, I'll go over and chat with him, and maybe I'll make a new best friend who is the owner of the sexiest voice in the history of mankind."

The maître d' brought us to our seats, and we worked our way through endless dishes of butter, cream, and pig fat. By now, Mr. Mason was dining at the very next table. Finally, the snotty, condescending, nose-in-the-air waiter brought a plate of little chocolate pastries and I asked for a cup of coffee.

"I am sorree, Madame, but we serve ze café *after* les petits four."

"Thank you, but I like my coffee *with* the dessert, please."

"Not posseeble."

"Couldn't you just make an exception this one little time?"

"Madame, I must inform you that in Frahnce, we do things differentlee from *your* kuntree."

And then I lost it, and I yelled at that snarky motherfucker, "Right! We actually *fought* the Nazis!"

James Mason stared as I was escorted out of the restaurant. We flew home the next day, and I was very glad to be back in the good old U.S. of A., where the customer is always right. Just to test it out, I went to a Broadway coffeeshop and asked for a liverwurst-and-peanut-butter sandwich. The waitress raised one eyebrow, then said, "Okay, doll, what kinda bread?"

10

EDIBLES (THE NOT-DRUG KIND)

What's cooking?

I Would Pay Extra for a House Without a Kitchen

How is it possible that I have only just discovered sweet Hawaiian rolls?

I am obsessed with food. When I can't sleep, I calm myself by designing this week's menus. While we're dining on roast chicken, I'm planning the next day's curried chicken salad. When I'm having my morning bagel, I think about tomorrow's breakfast blintzes. I collect recipes. I watch *Chopped* the way other people watch sporting events. I scream at the screen, "Watch out! Your sauce is separating and it's time to plate!" There is only one food-related activity that I have no interest in, and that's cooking.

I can put a meal together, thank you. I simply prefer not to. Remember that show *30 Minute Meals*? Who's got thirty minutes? Maybe I would feel differently if I had one of those kitchens in a Nancy Meyers movie. It's large, it's light, there are gleaming copper pans hanging next to a twelve-thousand-dollar six-burner Bertazzoni stove. There is a huge island, a four-door fridge, and every conceivable mixer, cooker, whisker, juicer, blender, chopper, coffeemaker, and processor. Plus, there is a large picture window overlooking a garden that is always sunny and always in bloom. That is not what I have.

What I have is a tiny room with almost no counter space and a view of nothing much. My four-burner stove is so poorly designed that I can only use two burners at a time. I have so little storage space that I have to keep extra wines in a box on the floor right next to the oven.

Truth be told, I have many friends who do not have that Ina Garten dream kitchen either, and yet they manage to get in there and slice and dice and sauté and whisk. They bake huge loaves of sourdough bread. They create their own stock out of veggie scraps that most people would throw out. They smoke their own salmon and make their own ricotta cheese. My response to all this is "Why???"

To them, being in the kitchen is relaxing and meditative. To me, it is about as relaxing as solitary confinement. Hold on a second! It *is* solitary confinement! Why would I choose to be trapped there when there's so much productive work I could be doing? I could be writing. I could be filming a TikTok. I could be playing Wordle.

A few years ago, I stupidly invited a small group for Thanksgiving dinner, and I stupidly decided to make everything from scratch. It took one week to prepare, and one week to bring the house and kitchen back to normal. Plus, the turkey was dry. Never again.

We can't afford to eat out every night, so how can I get food on the table with a minimum of effort? Here's one solution: salsa. Salsa is a magical ingredient that makes everything better, with no work. You want some guac? Just mash an avocado with some salsa. You want meatloaf? Just mix a pound of ground turkey with a jar of salsa. You want a spicy appetizer? Toss some ready-cooked shrimp with some salsa. You want some gazpacho? Just blend yesterday's leftover salad with some salsa. My next book after this one will be *The Two-Ingredient Salsa Cookbook*.

But my favorite kitchen time-saver is my husband. Several years ago, I announced that I was retiring from all food-preparation duties and that it was now his turn. I'm proud to say that Benni has stepped up to the (dinner) plate. He will throw together some grilled salmon, roasted garlic potatoes, and a tossed salad without complaining, and will even sort of clean up afterward. Sometimes you just get lucky.

Who Thought This Up?

I often wonder how humans started eating certain foods. Like artichokes. Who was the first person who said, "Methinks I'll take this prickly thistle, boil it, then scrape out the flesh of each leaf with my teeth, then remove those little hairs so I can get to the best part, the heart"?

I also wonder about those traditional food combos. They weren't traditional until someone tried it, and now we wouldn't have it any other way. I would never, ever eat a baked potato without sour cream and chives. And who got the genius idea to make a sandwich out of bacon, lettuce, tomato, and mayonnaise? (I add a little avocado, because I add a little avocado to everything. I have to; that's a law in California.)

Who said, "This raw fish with rice is okay, but it's a little on the bland side. Let's try adding some soy sauce and marinated ginger. Then, let's dig up this spicy wasabi rhizome and turn it into a paste to add a little pop"?

When I was a kid, I constructed my own delectable combo. I arranged some potato chips on a platter, then placed an M&M in the center of each chip, thus creating what I thought was a blissful blend of crisp and smooth, salty and sweet. Why has this not become a culinary classic?

> What did we do before prosecco?

"Restaurant" Is My Favorite Word

Is there anything better than ending the day by sitting outside in a cafe and enjoying some chips and guac and a margarita? I love restaurants. I love the whole ritual of getting dressed (this alone is a special treat for me, since I spend my life in sweats), joining friends, making choices, and enjoying dishes that I would never have the skill or patience to make at home.

I get so excited when we're going out, that I study the menu at home during the day so I can fantasize about different possibilities. Should I have the *linguine alle vongole* or the eggplant parm? Oh wait! Polenta with mushrooms! I love polenta! Should we start with arugula salad or calamari? I am salivating as I write this.

I knew a couple who were planning a trip to Europe, and made reservations at the hottest new five-star restaurants. Not me. I would never pay an obscene sum of money for moth-wing foam and sous vide mink entrails. My idea of a great eatery is a place where Grandma is in the kitchen, making the dishes *her* grandma made. You might then assume that I never eat fast food, but you would assume wrong. I'm not a purist; I have been known to crave the crunch of some KFC. Plus, I love French fries, and I love home fries, but what I love best are sweet potato fries.

Much as I enjoy eating out, we've had our fair share of disasters. One night we went to dinner with some new acquaintances. We let them pick the restaurant. They each had a lobster appetizer, rib roast, cappuccinos, and tiramisu. Benni and I had pasta, and we shared a salad.

When the bill came, the other couple said, "Shouldn't we just split it?" I'm usually not at a loss for words, but I honestly didn't know how to deal with that moment, so we grudgingly subsidized their pricy cholesterol. Next time, we'll pick the restaurant. I hope they like Vietnamese udon noodles; we have a local place that serves them for $10.99.

I Go on Oprah

I have a food compulsion: if someone else is paying, and I can have whatever I want, I just lose all control. It's like there's this tape in my brain that keeps playing over and over from my childhood: "Finish your plate! Little children in Europe are starving!" (Remember, I grew up a long time ago.) My friend Sandra Shapiro's mother used to say, "Eat whatever you want—and the rest, put in your mouth." What chance did I have?

I am so compulsive about not wasting food that when I see the anorexic young woman at the next table in the restaurant leaving over half of her lasagna, I have to fight the impulse to say, "Excuse me, but if you're done with that, would you mind passing it this way?"

My worst food disaster happened when I was a guest on *Oprah*... Once again, I'm so impressed with that statement that

I'm going to repeat it. My worst food disaster happened when I was a guest on *Oprah*. It started like this: People see me as your "typical Jewish woman," and maybe it's true. I've got curly hair and noisy opinions on every subject, and I have never owned a backpack. Plus, even after years of speech classes, I still have an unmistakable Bronxiness in my voice.

So, I'm stuck with being a living stereotype, and the worst thing about it has been having to spend my life suffering through the never-ending barrage of nasty jokes—told by Jewish men—about spoiled princesses and smothering mothers and frigid wives. "My doctor told me to avoid any excitement, so I married a Jewish woman." Ba-dum-bum.

So, I decided to write a book defending my team, because I see us as lively, earthy, and nurturing. I wrote to *The Oprah Winfrey Show* and suggested that they do an episode about "Ethnic Men Who Reject Their Own Women." Holy feces! They liked the subject, and I was invited to appear as an expert witness. Oh my God! I was going on *Oprah*! My life would never be the same. I was gonna be rich. I was gonna be famous!

Now let me explain why this is the thinking of a brain-damaged person. I didn't have a book. I didn't have a publisher. What I had was an idea for a book that I never did get around to writing. I am the only person in the history of the universe who went on *The Oprah Winfrey Show* with nothing to sell. All I had was a *complaint*.

Oprah flew me to Chicago, first class. Big mistake. Because, as I said, I have this problem with complimentary food. I was on the plane, and the attendant said, "Hi there! For your hors d'oeuvre, would you care for smoked salmon, artichoke dip, or paté?"

And I said, "Yes!" I followed all that with a stuffed Cornish game hen and a hot fudge sundae. I wobbled off the plane, and a limo whisked me to my luxurious hotel—just in time for dinner. Oprah Winfrey was trying to kill me.

I didn't feel so good. All my body really wanted was a nice cup of chamomile tea, but I told my body to mind its own damn business and sat down to a five-course meal with beef Stroganoff. (I don't usually eat red meat, but it's the most expensive thing on the menu.) My body was very angry with me. I just hoped those starving children in Europe were happy!

I was seriously unwell. I couldn't sleep. I was up all night. What was I going to say on the show tomorrow to convince people that Jewish women deserve some respect? At five-thirty, I got a wake-up call. I was sicker than ever, but breakfast arrived, and I forced down eggs Benedict and a stack of buttermilk pancakes. I had no choice; it was paid for! At six thirty, the limo arrived to take me, sick and nauseous, to the studio. It was showtime.

I was ushered into the green room—how appropriate. Oh no! There was a snack table! Fruit! Cheese! Chips! Nuts! Candy bars! I controlled myself and sampled only one of each. Then we went into the studio. The first speaker was a single Jewish professional man, and he spouted the usual garbage: "I never date Jewish women. They look alike; they think alike. The only thing they're interested in is the size of your wallet."

It was my turn to reply, and I wanted to bury this slimeball with my cutting wit and irresistible charm. But by now there were clumps of Stroganoff in Benedict sauce floating around in my esophagus, and I was about to represent Jewish women by vomiting in front of twenty-two million people.

I was so sick that my witty and charming response to this jerkwad was, "Same to you and double!"

So I failed big-time there. I had a chance to make a bold public statement about something I'm passionate about, but instead—just like every other addict who's ever lived—I chose gratification over happiness. My name is Annie, and I'm a foodaholic.

The next day, at home, Benni made his usual attempt to console me. "You're making too much of this. Who watches *Oprah* anyway?"

And then I heard my son talking on the phone. "No way, that wasn't my mother. I mean, not my real mother. You didn't know I was adopted?"

> Have you ever noticed that the more colorful food is, the tastier it is? If it's gray, stay away.

You know that expression, "There's no such thing as a free lunch?" I guess it's true.

Dumb Diets

Deep down, we all know that short-term extreme diets do not have any lasting effect. Deep down, we all know that the only way to lose weight permanently is to eat less and move more for the rest of your days. And yet we keep torturing ourselves with cray-cray fads that have zero scientific validity, like "detox cleanses" or the cabbage soup diet or going gluten-free for no rational reason.

When I was younger and less wise than I am now, I went on an agonizing pineapple diet, where I ate only pineapple for two days of the week. I suffered through this for several weeks, lost a little weight, and gained it right back—and more—as soon as

I went back to my regular diet of the five food groups: bread, potatoes, pasta, rice, and chocolate. I later learned that the person who created the pineapple diet was not a physician or nutritionist. He was just a guy who happened to love pineapple.

In Japan, there is a ritual of beginning each meal by saying, "*Hara hachi bu*," which means, "Eat until you are eighty percent full." This tradition originated in Okinawa, where people are among the longest-lived in the world, so "*hara hachi bu*" makes a lot of sense. Unfortunately, it wouldn't work for me.

I wonder how you say "120 percent" in Japanese.

My favorite Trader Joe's items:

Frozen onion soup
Peanut butter pretzels
Spicy hummus
Organic Persian cucumbers
Korma fish curry
Asparagus risotto

As I look at this list, I realize it could be served all at once for the perfect dinner.

Brits and Toast

I read a lot of English mysteries and watch a lot of English TV series, and I don't understand the Brits' addiction to toast. Toast for breakfast, toast for afternoon tea, toast for a snack. Toast is not food! It's just burned bread, and it's not a meal unless there's something tasty on it, like tuna salad or melted cheese.

Which brings us to *Downton Abbey*. I love that show, even though the affectionate relationship between upstairs and downstairs is a total crock. Aristocrats in those days were viciously cruel, and their servants lived wretched, brutal lives. But I don't mind some feel-good fiction, since real life is so often feel-bad.

Anyway, at one point, a member of the family finally wakes from a coma, and the imperious Maggie Smith says something like, "She hasn't eaten for days. She must be starving. Have cook prepare some toast!" What the hell is wrong with these people?

And it gets even scarier, because it seems that toast was considered medicinal in years gone by, so if you were sick, you were given a horror called a "toast sandwich." Here's the recipe from *Mrs. Beeton's Book of Household Management*: "Place a very thin piece of cold toast between two slices of thin bread-and-butter."

I'm so glad we won the Revolution.

11

WEARABLES

To spend or not to spend

Labels: What's in a Name?

I was walking in Santa Monica and passed a family with an adorable little girl who was wearing a T-shirt with a screaming Balenciaga logo. Really? A toddler shilling for a fashion label? I would call that child abuse.

I don't get the whole "label" thing. Why do you need the world to know who manufactured your suitcase? I will answer that. Because you need the world to know that you have money. A lot of status fashion isn't even particularly beautiful. Like that drab British Burberry stuff. Why would you pay $660 for a duller-than-dull tan, brown, and gray plaid scarf? Oh, wait, there's free shipping. I guess that makes it worth it.

There's a famous fashion dictum from Coco Chanel: "Before you leave the house, look in the mirror and remove one accessory." Coco Chanel was an anti-Semite, a homophobe, and a

Nazi collaborator. So, before I leave the house, I look in the mirror and add some accessories. Coco Chanel can suck my fashion dictum, and I would definitely never flaunt that CC logo unless I got an apology and a sizable donation to the ACLU.

There was an incident a while back in a Beverly Hills restaurant where a diner was robbed of his five-hundred-thousand-dollar Richard Mille wristwatch. I guess he couldn't afford the RM 56-02 Tourbillon Sapphire, which, "priced at over two million dollars, features a case forged from sapphire and the elegant, weightless nature of a tourbillon timepiece." What a loser.

If I had an extra half a million bucks lying around, I wouldn't squander it on a timepiece. I would use it to start a gun exchange program: you give me your weapon, and I will give you one month in the mountaintop Zen monastery of your choice.

> I always put on perfume before a Zoom call.

Misadventures of a Thriftaholic

Imelda Marcos collected three thousand pairs of shoes while her dictator husband was busy brutalizing his country. I, too, love to shop. And that's about all I have in common with Imelda. For one thing, my husband has never brutalized anyone—except when he tells me to calm down and act normal. For another thing, I never buy retail. My motto is, "Used is the new black."

I spend my life scouring thrift stores, estate sales, and flea markets. That way I can feel morally superior while satisfying my lust for goods. All kinds of goods: vintage costume jewelry, '50s harlequin sunglasses, embroidered wedding hankies—whatever. When I pick up a Sabatier carving knife for a buck, it's not only good for my limited budget, it's also a form of recycling. So I'm not just shopping; I'm saving the planet!

As with any obsession, there came a time when the pleasure turned to pain. Every closet, shelf, and drawer in the house was overflowing with valuable items that were never used. I don't use the silk Armani slacks, because I rarely get out of my pajamas. I don't use the Bakelite flatware, because I rarely entertain. Who's got time to entertain? I'm much too busy buying Bakelite flatware!

After a family intervention, I agreed to go cold turkey. Oh, I wouldn't give up treasure hunting, but I wouldn't keep anything. I would turn my compulsion into a business. I started selling my goodies—some on eBay, some to resale shops, some to private dealers.

I appreciated the extra income because, and this might come as a shock to you, as an actress/writer, I do not have steady employment. It was fun to have a little cottage industry but, like all entrepreneurs, I dreamed of The Big Score: the costume person from a film studio who would appreciate my exquisite taste and, since they were paying with someone else's dime, would never haggle over the price. I would then sit in the audience and think, "That's my 1950s cocktail dress! That's my signed Weiss necklace!"

And so, it came to pass. Twice a year we have a huge yard sale to unload the surplus goods. One day, a young woman named Phoebe Williams showed up and announced that she was doing wardrobe for a DreamWorks movie. Just like in my fantasy, Phoebe gushed over my fabulous taste, and phoned her assistant to check the sizes of various actors. She bought a flare rockabilly skirt and a '60s velvet blazer and a few beaded dresses and some vintage clip earrings. She was in a hurry to get back to the set, so I took a check for four hundred dollars. She promised to come over every month to check out my inventory. My dream had come true: I was in business with Steven Spielberg.

The check bounced. It wasn't just an oversight; the account had been closed for several months. I called DreamWorks and asked for Phoebe Williams. No such person. I called a few other studios. No luck. Phoebe Williams was a total fraud. The assistant she had been talking to was probably a dial tone. She'd played on my greed, my vanity, and my pathetic eagerness to be a professional shopper for the movies. My miracle had turned into a "be careful what you wish for" fable.

I was, of course, furious, but I was also fascinated by the psychopathology at work here. If you are a skilled con artist, why steal used goods from aging yentas at yard sales? Whatever happened to professional standards? Even criminals should aim high.

I started leaving phone messages for Phoebe, sometimes several in one day. No reply, of course. We drove to the address on the check. No such person, of course. You know how you can be obsessed with revenge fantasies over people who have done you wrong?

Like…oh, let's say, Harold, the forty-five-year-old boyfriend who leaves you for a twenty-five-year-old barista named Petunia, who doesn't see the point of voting. You run into him a year later in a tai chi class and say, "Hi, Harold—nice to see you. Gee, Petunia, sorry about that rash. Hey, let me introduce my fiancé, Brad Pitt!"

Or the college teacher who accused you of cheating because he didn't believe you were smart enough to have written that excellent term paper on Thomas Mann. You cross paths a decade later at the White House: "Excuse me, aren't you Professor Liebowitz? I wish I could stay and chat, but I'm late for a meeting upstairs in the Oval Office. Enjoy the tour!"

For many months, I kept thinking of all the things I would say to Phoebe Williams if I were to ever run into her. How I would make a loud scene in public, and Benni would be there, and we would force her to pay us back.

And so it came to pass. We walked into a wine shop not far from home, and there was Phoebe Williams, purchasing a magnum of Bollinger champagne and writing out a phony check in the same phony checkbook. And just like in my fantasies, I yelled to the owner, "Don't take that check! She's a con artist!"

Phoebe looked up and said, just as sweet as could be, "Oh, hi there! I'm so glad I found you. I've been looking all over for you. I think I owe you money!"

We walked Phoebe over to the ATM, and as she handed me the cash, she said, "I know you don't believe me, but I'm really a good person."

"Phoebe, every single thing you told me was a lie."

"No, I'm exactly what I said. I'm a studio executive."

If she had only put her mind to it, she probably could have been. She had all the qualifications.

I guess once in a very great while, miracles *do* happen! The miracle was that I got my money back from a con artist. And there was another miracle. I found a way to feel the teensiest bit of compassion for Phoebe Williams. Oh, I still hate that psycho bitch, and I don't forgive her crime. But sometimes I wonder about her life. I wonder how someone gets to be so wicked. I

> Some days, all I want to do is stay in the house with no bra and no makeup. By the end of the day, I'm so depressed that the only thing that cheers me up is to put on a bra and makeup and leave the house.

wonder if she enjoys close friendships, a loving partner, a warm family life, or meaningful work that she is passionate about. I seriously doubt it.

I'm lucky enough to have all those things. They are my most valued possessions, and no one can steal them from me.

Shopping as Meditation

When I rule the world, every public space will be a phone-free zone. Because stuff like this happens too often—I'm wandering through the clearance racks at TJ Maxx, which, for me, is an opportunity to practice mindfulness. I feel the fabrics...I study the price tags...I slip on the shoes...I'm approaching Nirvana.

Suddenly the calm mood is shattered by some young ditz-head whining into her phone. "Oh my God, like, I am totally exhausted. Plus, I just got my *period!*"

"Uh, excuse me? I wonder if you could lower your voice just a wee bit?"

"Why? What is this, a liberry?"

"No, I would just rather not hear about your bodily functions."

"Well, hellooo! Who is asking you to listen?"

I learned my lesson, and I've decided to change my tack. The next time my space is invaded by some nitwit's phone babble, I am simply going to join the conversation.

"I just got my period..." she'll say.

"Sorry to interrupt, but this is such a strange coincidence. I was just this moment thinking about my vagina!"

That ought to shut her up!

I want a simple cotton wireless bra, but all they have in the stores are padded polyester flotation devices.

12

HOUSE AND GARDEN

I want both

More Is More

am not a fan of good taste. For too many years now, the trend
in home decor has been the simplicity of midcentury design.
Clean lines, neutral shades, uncluttered surfaces. Thanks,
but no thanks. I spent a lot of time in Denmark when I got
married, so when I enter a space filled with muted Scandinavian
furnishings, it is a reminder of all those dreary, colorless homes
in 1964 Copenhagen.

I much prefer curvy lines, vivid graphics, and lots of kooky
objects from all over the world. I hate white walls; I hate beige
houses. People who live in beige houses have beige brains.
(I'm not exactly sure what beige brains are, but you get what
I'm saying.)

I will admit that those austere minimalist spaces can have a
pleasant sense of serenity. They suggest a peaceful setting for

meditation, like a Japanese temple. A Japanese temple is a nice place to visit, but I wouldn't want to live there.

As always, fashion goes through cycles, so now the new trend is maximalism. Wallpaper is coming back, even on ceilings. People want to live like I do, in a plush cocoon of color and patterns. What took them so long to catch up?

> I always make my bed first thing in the morning; passing an orderly bedroom during the day gives me a sense of comfort. I might, however, leave dirty dishes in the sink for many hours. I'm talking double digits. Nobody's perfect.

Neat and Tidy

For years, I've been collecting newspaper clippings that illustrate something I call The Neat and Tidy Syndrome. If a journalist describes your home as anything resembling "neat and tidy," that means he didn't expect it. Here are a few of my favorites. We'll begin with vicious killers.

The young immigrant suspected of murdering Bill Cosby's son "lived with his mother in a neat apartment…"

A Queens teenager accused of killing a Chinese restaurant owner for a free meal "was arrested outside his parents' neatly kept home…"

The infamous Ted Kaczynski's family lived in "a blue-collar Polish enclave of neat homes and tiny well-tended yards close to Kaczynski's Sausages."

I suppose it is surprising that violent lunatics grow up in orderly environments rather than moldy basements (although Kaczynski's Sausages sounds pretty grim to me). But apparently, it's also newsworthy that Black people live in clean homes. I read an interview with Maya Angelou that described her living room as "spic-and-span."

And I thought, "Huh? 'Spic and span?' It's Maya fucking Angelou! What did they expect? Rotting pizza boxes and crumpled beer cans?"

Another Black writer, Antwone Fisher, whose memoir, *Finding Fish*, was turned into a movie, "lives with his family in a sprawling, meticulously cared-for ranch house." Really? Meticulously cared-for? And he's not white? That's amazing!

The Neat and Tidies are usually poor or blue-collar. "Outside his tidy row house, [slain bus driver] Conrad Everton Johnson would play with his children…. He kept his car meticulously clean." A double whammy. Not only is this lowly bus driver's home tidy, but his car is clean. Can you believe it?

The houses in a Puerto Rican neighborhood in New York "are small and tidy." A mother and daughter were shot and killed in "the well-tended Reyes home."

Would any reporter describe a Kardashian home as "well-tended"? I think not. It's no news that very rich people live in spotless homes. That's because they can afford to pay poor people like Mrs. Reyes to scrub, vacuum, and dust. So why should anyone be surprised that those same people live in clean houses? They know how to do it right; they've had practice.

This lowly-but-neat syndrome is not just American. "From his modest but well-kept apartment in the impoverished Israeli town of Kiryat Malachi, [an Ethiopian Jew]…" Triple Grand Slam: an impoverished Black Jew has a well-kept home!

And it's not just the dwellings that are immaculate. Former prison inmates "are well dressed, some in business suits. Janice is wearing a bowler hat decorated with flowers. One of the women stands with her son, a smart-looking boy...in a stiff blue suit."

"Well dressed" is not used to describe rich people, and the floral hat and stiff blue suit are a not-so-subtle way of letting us know that we're talking about low-class folks here.

So, here's my dilemma: what should I do if a journalist wants to come to my house for an interview? If I straighten up the clutter, I risk making it into the Neat and Tidy file and then people will think I'm poor, or Black, or a murderer. I think I'll suggest meeting in a coffeeshop—and I'll take care not to be too well-dressed.

We went to Costco and got hearing aids, two computers, and a roast chicken.

Gardening Tips from Someone with a Black Thumb

I love having a garden. I love flowers and fruit trees and home-grown herbs and the welcoming fragrance of a blossoming vine at the front door. The only problem is, my gardening skills are on a par with my cooking skills. I stink at digging, weeding, staking, or transplanting, and I don't really enjoy bending down, lifting things, or getting my hands dirty.

And Benni is no better. He once proudly showed me a patch of succulents he had put in all by himself, totally clueless that he had put them in upside down, with their roots waving merrily in the air.

And yet, with the help of the strapping teenage boy next door, we do manage to grow things—mostly because in this benevolent Southern California climate, all you have to do is stick a plant in the ground and add a little water to create a life.

As usual, I try to keep the cost down. A lot of my treasured plants began as cuttings or exchanges from other gardeners. The most spectacular of those is a night-blooming cereus that originated on my buddy Kene's grandmother's terrace in Puerto Rico forty years ago. I continue that legacy by giving away cuttings to friends and neighbors. It's the gift that keeps on giving, at my favorite price of zero.

And then there are the rescues. Wherever I go, I look for teeny bits and pieces of plants that have broken off and are just lying on the ground. I have scavenged countless abandoned succulents and geraniums on residential streets, in front of restaurants, and in the courtyards of fancy medical buildings. I have now fostered enough agave plants to make a case of tequila.

I've known some really talented gardeners. One friend had a bougainvillea vine blooming on the walls of her dining room in Massachusetts; another grew a lemon tree in his Connecticut kitchen and harvested fruit on a snowy winter day. But the plant people I admire most are those guerilla growers like that genius fashion designer Ron Finley, who turns abandoned, garbage-filled urban lots in South Central L.A. into places of beauty, nourishment, and civic pride. I don't know about you, but I'm a big fan of beauty, nourishment, and civic pride.

13

THE GEEZER YEARS

Not so terrible

My Fifteen Minutes

So this funny thing happened one day: I almost died. Around twenty years ago, we went out with friends just before Labor Day weekend, and the next day I had an upset stomach, which I ascribed to eating and drinking too much, because I'm always eating and drinking too much. Suddenly I went hot and woozy and collapsed onto the bathroom floor.

The ambulance came, and a quartet of studly EMT guys did an impressive piece of choreography as they shoved furniture out of the way of the gurney. I kept telling them how kind they were, which was my pathetic way of flirting.

We got to the emergency room at Cedars Sinai L.A., and I was immediately diagnosed with internal bleeding and shipped off to the intensive care unit. The ICU was in the Marvin Davis

Tower, or the Steven Spielberg Institute, or the David Geffen Hall—whatever. (Remember, this is Los Angeles, where it's all about *credits*.)

At this point, my vital signs were so low, they were unreadable. Benni told me afterward that my skin was the color of wax paper. In udda woids, I was dying—which really didn't feel all that bad, because when you're that weak, you just relax and surrender to the moment—kinda like being on nitrous oxide, my personal drug of choice.

I got a blood transfusion, under protest, after being assured that my chances of contracting a disease from it were one in three hundred thousand. I did not find those odds comforting.

By now I had been checked by several beautiful, young, Asian women doctors who were all named Nguyen. Enter the big gun: the gastroenterologist, Shahab Mehdizadeh, twelve years old. He told me I maybe had a bleeding ulcer, which he could maybe fix the next day, if they can maybe find a staff to work on Labor Day. But he kept staring at me in a weird way and finally said, "You look so familiar. I know you from somewhere…" So, I asked him if he ever watched *Seinfeld*.

"Oh my God, I just saw you last night!" he said. "You're Doris Klompus!"

From then on, the Filipino nurses on the floor all referred to me as "Mrs. Annie Korzen, famous actress." And who was I to disillusion them? They seemed to consider it an honor to sponge my face and wipe my behind. To be fair, I don't think my "celebrity status" got me any special treatment. They just happened to be gentle souls who did stinky, smelly, and underpaid work with grace and humanity. I thanked them whenever I could manage to open my cotton-dry mouth—partly because

I was sincerely grateful, and partly because I figured that when your life depends on other people, it might be a good idea to be courteous. (I never understand those dopes who are rude to waiters; they are alone in the kitchen with your food!)

Nurse Mary Bell from Manila came in, closed the door, and whispered, "Would you like to hear some gossip?"

Now, I had been lying flat on my back for two days with tubes in both arms. Not allowed to eat or drink, not even water, couldn't poop without an audience, couldn't read or do crosswords or talk on the phone. And there was no DVR with a million titles, so I was forced to watch live TV. I saw three crime shows in a row that featured female victims who were raped and mutilated and, you know, the fun of that wears off after a while. So yeah, I was ready to hear some gossip.

"We have been talking in the nurses' station, and we have all decided that Mrs. Annie Korzen, famous actress, is the nicest patient in the ICU."

And I burst out crying. I cried because, like Sally Field, I am always moved when people like me. I cried because winning a popularity contest in a hospital ward had never been on my wish list of prizes I would like to win. But most of all, I cried because they probably always give the Miss ICU award to the patient who is terminal and doesn't know it yet.

Nurse Mary Bell was so upset by my tears that she took my hands and kindly asked if I would like her to pray with me, which made me blubber even louder. Even if I were a prayerful person, I wouldn't have known what to say. "Please God, don't let me die! I wanna live!" is so lame.

Three days later, I was having dinner on the beach with darling Benni. It seemed my ulcer probably had been caused by

Shooting Blanks

I get some of my best ideas when I'm away from my desk, which is a good excuse for leaving the computer as often as possible. I ruminate as I stroll in the park, I fantasize as I do water-walking in the pool, I get flashes of inspiration as I examine the peaches at the farmers' market. And then I promptly forget everything. The rest of this section will be left blank, as an homage to lost gems. May their memory be a blessing. What memory?

Chinese herbs, which I'd been taking to stay healthy, or aspirin therapy, which I also had been taking to stay healthy. Baby Shahab and his team of first-generation and immigrant women fixed me up just fine, but it was kinda humiliating that a near-death experience was the result of self-care.

Fun Funerals

I have been to quite a few "celebrations of life," and I'm here to tell you that for a really good time, you have to go to a showbiz funeral. That's because the speeches are written and spoken by people who are very good at writing and speaking.

Quite a few years ago, our neighbor Dick O'Neill died. He was a well-respected character actor, so the memorial service was held on the Paramount Studios lot. An impressive lineup of film and TV luminaries spoke, and the service was sprinkled with film clips of Dick's career. We couldn't attend, so a few months later, Dick's widow came over and played us a video of the event. She laughed again at every witty anecdote and cried again at every tender recollection. Clearly, rewatching the service was a healing experience for her, and it reminded me that funerals are not for the dead; they are for the living.

And as so often happens—at least in this book—you don't have to follow any rules. There are all kinds of ways to honor the dead. My friend Mandy shocked everyone by having her husband's memorial service in a nightclub. We danced to Rob's favorite swing band and enjoyed the vino he especially liked. *Dancing* at a funeral? Why not? It was a fitting tribute to a wine collector who loved to jitterbug.

When my mother-in-law, Mia, died, the family invited a violinist to perform at the funeral. He played on Mia's fine old violin. She had sold it to him for much less than it was worth, because she admired his talent. Again, a fitting tribute.

And now we come to me, and my own demise. My main problem with dying is all the stuff I'll be missing: my invitation to host *SNL*, my grandson's presidential inauguration, and... my funeral. But wait! Why should my survivors have all the fun? Haven't I earned the right to attend that one last party?

When we know the end is coming, Benni and I will invite a huge crowd. I will plan the menu (dim sum and Bellinis); choose the speakers; book the local high school chorus to sing Bach, the Beatles, and Leonard Cohen; and write the eulogy for Benni.

It's always good to have an exit strategy.

There are a lot of advantages to being young, but you can't beat those senior discounts.

Age Gap

There is definitely a schism between me and anyone under sixty, and here is a list of some of our differences, starting with phone use. If you want to give me a brain aneurism, ask me to text you a screenshot. I'm not a total Luddite; I happily use my trusty iPhone 8 to check emails while I'm in line at Goodwill, I use Waze to avoid traffic jams, and I relax with Words with Friends.

But younger people use their phones every single moment of their lives, for every single thing in their lives, including stuff I could never enjoy on that tiny screen, like reading a book or watching a movie. Plus, they record events instead of fully experiencing them. You're at a Paul McCartney concert. You've got the real thing in front of you, in person and on giant screens, but you spend the whole evening with your hand raised, watching him through your teensy phone. Why? I don't get it. After this event, will there be no other coverage available of Sir Paul? Do you feel it is your sole responsibility to preserve this event for posterity?

But what I resent most about your always being on your phone is that it prevents me from talking to you. I can no longer strike up conversations on airplanes, on supermarket checkout lines, in nail salons, or just sitting on a park bench. These days, chatting up a stranger would make me an annoying old lady, which I guess I am, but I'm an annoying old lady who occasionally has something interesting to say, so you might be missing out, bubba!

Seniors don't frequent Starbucks the addictive way the juniors do. I'm not much of a cook, but even I can boil some water and froth some milk for my morning cinnamon latte. It costs a helluva lot less than four bucks, and I'm not destroying the planet with those throw-away cups.

Young people have frequent casual sex. I miss that. They enjoy the thrill of a first-time hook-up. I miss that. They float on the cloud of a new romantic liaison. I miss that. But here's what I do have: as a long-married woman, I get to share my bed with someone without worrying if this relationship has a future, and without obsessing about that worry nonstop night and day with my friends, my family, my coworkers, my neighbors, and the pizza delivery guy.

Young women suffer through the agony of skin-tight jeans and crippling high heels, while lucky old me can luxuriate in the heavenly comfort of elastic-waist pants and socks with sandals.

Young people need to be popular. When I was a young person, I did a show where the rest of the cast hated me. If I mentioned a book I liked, they would exchange annoyed looks. If I never heard of the band they were talking about, they would exchange annoyed looks. At meals between shows, no one wanted to sit with me, and I cried myself to sleep every night. Since that time, I've been a member of several theater companies and storytelling groups, where I have formed loving, lasting, friendships with people I admire and respect. Why did I care so much about pleasing people that I didn't really like that much? They were dull. They were superficial. They were intellectual lightweights. I cared because youngsters have a need to be liked, while worldly, wise oldsters like me don't give a shit.

This not-giving-a-shitness has enabled me to say no, which I couldn't do when I was younger. I once foolishly agreed to spend a weekend camping in the Adirondacks, because I didn't want people to know that I'm afraid of nature. I couldn't find my way to the latrine in the middle of the night, so I wiped myself with a leaf, and ended up with poison ivy on my vajayjay.

At college, I foolishly agreed to lend my valuable Martin guitar to a girl I hated, because she was very popular and I didn't want everyone to know I hated her. She ended up "accidentally" dropping the guitar, and it was ruined forever. She did not offer to replace it.

As a young wife, I foolishly agreed to allow a very "distinguished" Danish poet to spend the weekend with us in New York. He turned out to be a very undistinguished raging alcoholic and passed out at the table during each meal. He then asked if he could stay a few more days, and I said yes because I didn't want him to know how much I hated having him there.

None of these disasters would happen now. With the self-assuredness of who-gives-a-fig geezerhood, I just smile sweetly, and say, "I'm so sorry, but I'm not really comfortable with that." It has taken me long time to learn those words, and I'm constantly amazed by the folks who never do—like all those passive dupes in the *Borat* movies.

Why I Hate Young People

Years ago, we were in Copenhagen and saw a huge billboard featuring an attractive older white-haired couple. They were both naked from the waist up, and the man was standing behind the woman with his hands partially covering her bare breasts. The tagline read: "Veuve Clicquot: For Those Special Occasions." You will not see that billboard anytime soon in Times Square. Americans are repulsed by the idea of seniors having sex, and they prefer to think that it never happens, which is just another delusional American myth. It's like believing that Columbus discovered America or that this is a land of equal opportunity.

Now that I'm a senior, let me tell you that emotionally, I'm the same person I was when I was sixteen. I think about boys, and I hate my hair. Getting old seems to have happened while my back was turned, and the challenges take some getting used to—like the insults.

We were in a restaurant, and the waiter said to Benni, "Would you care for a cocktail, sir?" And then he turned to me and said, "And how 'bout you, young lady?" Let me tell you one thing I do not need in my life: I do not need to be condescended to by unemployed actors. So, when I turned seventy, I decided not to lie about it, or to apologize for it, but to celebrate it. We invited about thirty-five people for an evening of dinner, dancing, songs, skits, and speeches—all about me and how wonderful I am. The guests were smart and funny and accomplished, including someone whose sister is best friends with a Tony winner.

The only sour note was when the young waiter handed me a glass of champagne and said, "Here you go, young lady." I lifted my glass, smiled graciously, and said, "Thanks, kid."

Younger people may make me feel undesirable and under-valued and unimportant, but I wouldn't want their life: "I wanna meet someone. I wanna nice place to live. I want interesting work. I'm so bored. I'm so lonely." I've got the answer to all those problems: grow old.

P.S. Remember when that jet had to land in the Hudson River? The flight crew who got all the passengers safely out of the plane consisted of three women aged fifty-one, fifty-seven, and fifty-eight. They were mature, experienced professionals who'd been drilled in this kind of emergency evacuation once a year, so between the three of them, they had practiced it ninety-two times. Lemme tell you something: the next time I book a trip, I am going to ask the average age of the crew. And if it's a bunch of inexperienced thirtysomethings, I ain't gettin' on that plane.

Why I Love Young People

From early childhood, every girl knows if she's pretty or not. I knew I was not. The pretty ones worked their good looks to obtain the teacher's kindness, to date the most popular guys, and to further their careers. I viewed their success with stinky jealousy and thought, "Why not me?" Now I'm beginning to see that I may have been the lucky one. Those beautiful women have been used and abused and exploited in all kinds of creepy-crawly ways, and the younger ones have finally decided to speak up.

I applaud their audacity, although the ferocity of the young PC crowd is a little scary. They're so grim. They're so angry. They're so humorless. Don't be so woke that you can't take a joke—or what's stupidly meant as a joke. There's a difference between predatory sexual abuse and plain old everyday obnoxious male behavior. Some fool who thinks he's being funny or flirty—and lacks the brain cells to know that he's being odious—should be reported and called out for his dumb dick behavior, but he shouldn't have his entire career canceled. Let the punishment fit the crime!

The young morals police can be just as ridiculously harsh on other subjects. I posted a TikTok of me devouring a nachos grande, and I got a comment accusing me of "cultural appropriation." Wha? You mean only French people can chew baguettes, and only the Chinese are allowed to have fried rice?

And now they're removing "offensive" words from children's books. That's totally shockingly scary. As I write this, I don't have a title for this book yet, but I fear my first choice of *Fat Ugly Crazy Retard* is not going to make the cut.

But here's the good news: yes, they often go too far, but these pesky young activists genuinely *care* about stuff—not just women's rights but all those other Big Bad Issues, like the environment, and racism, and homelessness, etc. etc. etc. And they care enough to organize, and make some noise, and try and make the stupid fucking world a better place—so I forgive them their irksome solemnity.

I have a more personal reason for liking the juniors. Before I got my blue check mark on TikTok that verified me as a social media biggie, I always assumed that being a mature, Jewish woman, I had a limited audience of mature, Jewish women. I couldn't have been more wrong. Some of my most devoted fans are Gen Zers, or college students, or even high school students, of assorted non-Yewish backgrounds. And they are all out of their bleeping minds.

They leave these nutsy, worshipful comments on my posts calling me "queen" and "icon." They tell me that I'm beautiful, which is a new experience for me. They tell me that they love my insights, and that they would like to be my neighbor, my child, my bestie. My favorite was, "I am astounded at how well I relate to an American Jewish woman in her eighties. I am a sixteen-year-old Afghan boy."

What the fuck is wrong with these youthful generations? Don't they know that I'm just a big-mouthed, big-nosed, nobody? Don't they know that I have been constantly reviled for being old, and opinionated, and ugly-Jewy-looking? How can they be seeing something attractive and valuable in me that the world has never noticed? Could it possibly be that they are right, and that I am better-looking and more likeable than I've been led to believe? Could it possibly be that humans are evolving into being more tolerant? Less sexist? Less bigoted? Less ageist?

That's probably the most optimistic thought I've ever had in my life, and I gotta say, having an optimistic thought is a nice new feeling. So thanks, kids!

ACKNOWLEDGMENTS

I have to thank my agent, Julia Lord, and my editor, Elena Vega, both of whom offered the support and encouragement that every writer craves. Ronda Spinak and Susan Morgenstern at the Braid Theater in Los Angeles, and Catherine Burns and Sarah Austin Jenness at The Moth, all helped me develop my storytelling skills. The amazing Penny Stallings gave me a zillion helpful notes, and Doug Field badgered me into trying my best. Iris Krasnow, Senior Editor of *The Ethel*, inspired me to keep writing, and Susanna Briselli gets hugs for creating the cover portrait. Last, and certainly most, is my heroic husband, Benni, who not only puts up with me but never stops cheering me on.

ABOUT THE AUTHOR

Annie Korzen played the recurring role of Doris Klompus on *Seinfeld* and many other character roles for TV and film, and has recently become a TikTok sensation with millions of views. She has written humorous essays for the *New York Times*, the *Los Angeles Times*, and other publications, as well as performed solo shows on three continents and toured the U.S. with The Moth Mainstage. Annie has been a guest on *Oprah*, *Access Daily*, *Inside Edition*, the *CBS Evening News*, and *Dr. Phil*.